Dazzled

DATE DUE

Back Again

D*azZled to Fr*azZled and Back Again

The Bride's Survival Guide

GINGER KOLBABA

Fleming H. Revell
A Division of Baker Book House Co
Grand Rapids, Michigan 49516

© 2004 by Ginger Kolbaba

Published by Fleming H. Revell
a division of Baker Book House Company
P.O. Box 6287, Grand Rapids, MI 49516-6287
www.bakerbooks.com

Printed in the United States of America

Library of Congress Cataloging-in-Publication Data
Kolbaba, Ginger.
    Dazzled to frazzled and back again : the bride's survival guide / Ginger
Kolbaba.
        p.   cm.
    Includes bibliographical references.
    ISBN 0-8007-5863-3 (pbk.)
    1. Wedding etiquette. 2. Weddings—Planning. I Title.
BJ2051.K65 2004
395.2′2—dc22   2003022208

Contents

Introduction

Welcome to Club Wed!

You're engaged and there's going to be a wedding! Congratulations are definitely in order. Soon you will be called "Mrs." You have just entered one of the most exciting times in your life. During this short period of time — and you'll find out how minimal a time span it is! — between becoming engaged and getting married, you will experience special privileges, some of which you will never experience again. For instance, you can walk into any room wearing that diamond and people will know you're engaged. You now get to say, "My fiancé," instead of calling your beloved, "My boyfriend." As in, "Hi, I don't know if you've met my fiancé. I've told my fiancé so much about you. My fiancé is such a wonderful person. Aren't you, Fiancé?" In addition, you can stare at your ring as much as and for as long as you like. (What's especially great is to move your ring around until it catches the light just right and makes a reflection on the wall.) Or you can spend hours writing your first name with your new last name. You can stand tall knowing the phrase, "Always a bridesmaid, never a bride," no longer applies to you. And with the way most bridesmaid dresses look, that alone is worth celebrating.

So celebrate! You've earned that ring. And the fun is about to begin. As my friend Jeane says, "This is one time in life when everything should stop to acknowledge there's a wedding." You will be pampered, primped, and prettied. You will feel like a princess. You will be the center of attention, the *bride*.

And if you're like every other bride, you are about to embark on the quest for the "perfect" wedding.

From the moment my beloved Scott slipped a diamond ring on my finger, I was walking down the aisle of my local bookstore browsing for the perfect wedding planner book. Actually, I purchased an assortment of perfect wedding books and magazines. (If you want to get "buff" by your wedding, just heft a few of those wedding magazines around.) I grabbed everything from Martha Stewart's book and magazine to *Weddings for Dummies*. I ran the gamut to insure my wedding day would be perfect. I studied how to have the ideal wedding — something I'd already been doing from the time I was nine years old. And since I married at thirty-two, I had been to more than my share of weddings — and definitely been *in* more than my share! — and I knew what I wanted to achieve and what I wanted to avoid at all costs. I did all the right things the books and "experts" advised. My expectations were high. Yes, this would be the perfect wedding — even if it killed me.

But soon into my journey through the engagement period, I discovered I needed a book that was titled *The Bride's Head Revisited . . . and Other Stuff You Need to Do When Preparing for a Wedding and Subsequent Marriage*. Unfortunately, that book doesn't exist. Instead, every book played into the romance of the occasion — without telling me the funny, poignant, and sometimes teary-eyed truth. I discovered that no book, magazine, or expert told me what to *really* plan for and expect. Namely, there is no such thing as a perfect wedding — or perfect engagement period, or perfect honeymoon.

While they informed me in which week I should order the invitations, how I should address them, the proper etiquette of who stands where in the receiving line, and which photographs to make sure the photographer takes, they neglected to tell me certain other what I'd deem "in the know" information. No one told me, for instance, that I'd ride an emotional roller coaster that left me ecstatic, weary, joy-filled, frustrated, and teary—sometimes all within the same afternoon. I didn't realize I would experience overwhelming stress or that the bridal boutiques are a billion-dollar industry and you are only as good as the dollars you shell out. Nor did I have any idea that it wasn't simply the books, magazines, and Martha Stewart who could guide me with their "expertise" to the perfect wedding. Oh no, I found dozens of "expert Martha Stewarts" who were more than happy to share their "wisdom," thoughts, opinions, and advice—all unsolicited, of course, and all "correct." I thought I was the only bride to be emotional, to experience doubts, and to argue with my fiancé over inane things such as which table setting we should put in our bridal registry. I spent many nights crying out to God, pleading, "I thought this was supposed to be a happy occasion—what's the deal? Is this a sign?"

One day at work while discussing wedding plans with several other engaged or newly wedded gals, I hesitatingly mentioned my struggles. I was positive they would look at me aghast, then declare they'd never felt that way. Boy, was I surprised. One woman said, "You too? I thought it was just me!" Another said, "Yeah, I thought there was something seriously wrong with me." What a relief to know I wasn't alone. What a double relief to know I was normal!

What was even more interesting was that as I began to tell people I was writing a book on what to expect when you're planning a wedding, everyone had an experience to share. They would lift their hand, roll their eyes, and say, "I've got a story for you!" Then they would narrate the incident, and I'd think, *They're right! That* is *a story.*

In his book *It Was on Fire When I Lay Down on It*, author Robert Fulghum sums up the nuptial celebration best: "Weddings seem to be magnets for mishaps and for whatever craziness lurks in family closets. In more ways than one, weddings bring out the ding-dong in everybody involved."[1]

That's why I'm writing this book. Well, that and because this is my therapy to help me recover from my wedding preparation experiences. But I digress. What you will experience in the coming months, just about every bride has experienced. And you too are normal.

Really, this book is about expectations. And while great expectations are good to have — they are the standard or the bar that is set — weddings, at some level, fall short of those desires. I was discussing wedding expectations with newlywed Christian singer/songwriter Nichole Nordeman recently. She said, "When I was planning my wedding, everyone kept asking me if I felt overwhelmed or stressed. And I could say honestly I was doing well. I didn't know what the big deal was. But, of course, I spoke too soon. About a month before my wedding, I got a panicked call from my seamstress who informed me that while she was pressing my gown, she burnt a hole in it — right in the front of the dress. At that moment, stress was an understatement!"

I'm not suggesting, of course, that brides shouldn't have certain expectations. We should! This is one of the most important events in a woman's life. However, in my experience, I discovered how easy it became to allow those expectations to grow into despots, never letting me rest, keeping me up at night, giving me nightmares and ulcers from anxiety. It's easy to slip into obsessing over what could go wrong. Yet the joy is to acknowledge those expectations and then say, "Regardless of what happens, I choose to let go of those things I cannot control and find pleasure in every situation."

I wish someone would have sat down with me after I became engaged and said, "Ginger, let's talk about what kind of expectations you have." Hopefully, this book will be that encouraging friend to help you navigate the endless series of jumbles that will make up your engagement, wedding, and honeymoon.

This book is not a how-to or a wedding planner/etiquette book. There are plenty of great ones already on the market. Instead, through the pages of this book you'll discover how to enjoy to the fullest this short period of life. You will prepare for the days after the honeymoon—when there is no more star treatment, and when the reality sinks in that you have a gazillion thank-you cards to write. You will discern how to separate which expectations are realistic, which ones are so far in fantasyland you need Pinocchio's nose to help you sort them out, and which ones you can hold on to for great stories years down the road. Finally, you can find "Quick Tips" in each chapter—advice from those brides who have been there, done that, and want to spare you from the same.

I've interviewed dozens of brides who honestly, genuinely, and courageously shared their experiences and what they learned. Because of the nature of their stories, most of the names have been changed in this book. While all the stories are true, many of these vulnerable women still maintain a relationship with their parents, in-laws, friends, and husbands—and would like to keep it that way. Myself included.

Please be assured I do not share any of these stories to shock, scare, or depress you. My goal is to prepare you for the unexpected. And trust me, you will experience the unexpected! I want to place a little reminder in your mind that will *ding!* when something unforeseen occurs, and you'll remember you are not alone. Hopefully, you will be better equipped to handle those times, and then, all importantly, to move on without them becoming major sticking points.

Regardless of your expectations and which ones are met and which aren't, you will love your wedding day. It will fill you with warm, wonderful memories—as long as you go into it with eyes wide open to the fact that something, somewhere is going to happen to test your "perfection" meter.

Finally, I want to thank the people who helped make this book possible. Thank you, Mom and Dad, for being great parents — particularly during those struggles with my inner bride. Thanks to all the women who have vulnerably shared their stories with me. That was a brave thing to do, especially knowing the stories might show up in print. And thank you, my precious husband, Scott, for marrying me. If you hadn't, I wouldn't have written this book. Instead, I would have written a book on how to be a happy single woman.

Now, may I be the first to offer you this hope for your journey: "May the LORD bless you and protect you. May the LORD smile on you and be gracious to you. May the LORD show you his favor and give you his peace" (Numbers 6:24–26).

Welcome to this new stage in your life. Welcome to the exclusive Club Wed! May this time bring every good and wonderful experience to you, your fiancé, and your inner bride!

Ginger McFarland Kolbaba,
married November 4, 2000

Part 1

Your Engagement

ONE

You're Engaged!
Now What?

The night was perfect. Holding out a single rose, Scott picked me up at my apartment. Then we drove to downtown Chicago. After we ate at a dimly lit, romantic, and overpriced fondue restaurant, we walked along Lake Michigan. Then we hopped into a horse-drawn carriage, and to the tune of the horses' clippity-clops, Scott bent on one knee, removed a box from his pocket, and took my hand. This was it!

Holding my hand, Scott began his prepared speech about finding someone with whom he could share his life, someone with whom he could grow old, someone who completed him. At least I think that was what he said. The longer he talked, the more I wanted what was in that box!

Finally! He opened the lid to reveal a beautiful diamond ring. When he asked, "Will you marry me?" I responded delightedly, "Yes! Yes, yes, yes!"

But soon I discovered there was a problem with our engagement. Namely, that while Scott had proposed, he just couldn't seem to sit still long enough for us to pick a date. Finally after several months, I came to a realization: Scott wasn't going to pick a date. So back went the ring into the box.

The second proposal was not nearly as romantic. No rose this time. No romantic dinner. Actually, we took a walk and it started to rain, so we ran under a picnic shelter. *This* was when he decided to present his soliloquy again. But this time it stuck, and he was ready to set the date. And no skidding heels this time. His second proposal came on July 30. He wanted to get married that fall — in October or November.

This time I would have been as excited about finding an oxygen tank to help me breathe as I was about finding the ring on my finger again. *Two and a half months to prepare a wedding?* my mind screamed.

"Are you serious?" I was finally able to gasp out. "You're joking, right? Right? I mean, do you have any idea how long it takes to plan a wedding? Most wedding experts suggest a minimum of a year. A minimum!"

Scott just looked at me with this blank look.

"How hard can it be?" he asked.

How hard can it be? *How hard can it be?!*

Amateur.

That day I called my parents to share the news. "But, Mom," I cried. "Scott thinks we can get married this year yet!"

"I'll help you. Don't worry about it," she offered graciously.

That Monday I had lunch with my friend Ramona who gave me one of the best pieces of advice about wedding planning I have heard. She listened patiently to my saga, then said, "My husband and I got married in three months. This is how I looked at it: You're going to have a lot of stress through the upcoming months. You need to decide if you want the stress stretched out over a year or compounded into a few months. You're going to be stressed either way."

Later that day a coworker, Theresa, mentioned that a friend of hers had gotten married in ten weeks. "Nobody told her they *couldn't* do a wedding in ten weeks," she said.

So that night I called Scott. "Okay," I said, still tentative about my decision, "let's do it."

And thus began the whirlwind of preparation.

Stress!

Recently I was speaking with a coworker who informed me she wasn't really stressed during her engagement period. I chuckled while I thought, *She has obviously deceived herself into forgetting that period of her life.* I was right. The longer we talked, the more her memories became clear. "Oh my," she admitted, "I guess I did have some stressful moments."

And who wouldn't? After all, this is one of the most important events of your life. Not only are you changing your life's course by entering into a legal, sacred, committed relationship in front of

Shine Language

Let's face it, it "don't mean a thing if you can't flaunt that ring." Here are six moves *Mademoiselle* magazine suggests to display your diamond.

The "hmmm": Plan "impromptu" pensive moments. Stroke your chin broodingly — until someone *oohs* at your ring.

The "contact lens": Even if you don't wear them, adjust lenses constantly. If you poke your eye out, at least you'll be glittering.

The "ohmigosh!": Express delighted astonishment while fluttering hand near cheek — at everything from memos to gruel.

The "tidy brow": Now that you have a ring to show off, it's very, very important to make sure you're properly groomed.

The "shades slide": Step one: grease nose. Step two: let gravity take its course. Step three: sigh, push up glasses, sparkle.

The "tender tuck": Choose products guaranteed to deliver flyaway hair. Secure tendrils behind ear. Repeat ad nauseam.[1]

God and your closest family and friends, but you're also throwing the biggest party you'll ever have to plan. It's okay to be frazzled. As a matter of fact, according to psychotherapist Linda Barbanel in her article "The Five Stages of Engagement" for *Mademoiselle* magazine: "The engagement period is a crisis time. Your emotions are running wild."[2]

You'll be amazed as you watch yourself, an otherwise level-headed woman, become completely overwhelmed by the rigors of planning this nuptial soiree. In short, your inner bride takes hold of your brain and screams, "This MUST be the *perfect* day!"

Quiz:
Are You an Overachieving Bride?

You may be one if you:

- invite opera diva Sarah Brightman to your wedding to sing—and honestly believe she'll come
- have a bridal party larger than the guest list
- expect each flower at your reception to be hand-opened
- plan to have three ceremonies so all your invited guests will make at least one
- arrange to have a samba parade in which each member of the bridal party plays an instrument and dances through your town
- rent a glass carriage shaped like a pumpkin to take you to your reception
- ask your guests to wear cream and beige to accentuate the setting—and your wedding colors

If you've answered yes to any of these, don't fret; you're not alone. Believe it or not, there are brides who actually did the above—and lived to tell about it.

Whether your engagement lasts two years or two months, you have a lot of planning to do. At some point you will probably feel as if you have been sucked into a whirlwind over which you have little or no control: the hundreds of details to which you must attend, the seas of fabric, the seemingly endless sources of to-do list anxiety.

If my mom and several friends hadn't stepped up to the plate to help, I couldn't have done it. Which brings me to my first, most important piece of advice: *Delegate*. If you don't learn that trick, you'll end up under a psychiatrist's care in a mental hospital — or you'll end up in prison.

Your Wedding Timeline

Finally! You've got the man, you've got the ring, you've set the date. Now what?

You need a timeline. The timelines that wedding books present are designed to help you get organized so your preparation process will flow smoothly. But have you looked at those timelines? I mean *really* looked at them? If you did everything they suggest, it would take you about three years before you could walk down the aisle.

If you doubt me, here's a timeline I compiled from several wedding planners. However, this one also includes the *real* (sometimes funny, sometimes nerve-wracking) story of what you need to do or what will happen to you in the months leading up to your day of bliss and euphoria.

This timeline is set for six to twelve months — that's the average length of most engagements. You may have set your wedding for a year and a half to two years away (stretch out the timeline) or you may have set your wedding for two months from now (in which case you'll combine most of the weeks and you will want to buy a bottle of extra strength aspirin right after reading this chapter).

19

Six to Twelve Months before the Wedding

Announce your engagement to everyone you know and then some — cashiers, stock boys, waitresses, bus drivers, phone operators. Call your Aunt Edith with whom you haven't spoken in five years to share the news.

If you or your fiancé have not met the other's parents and/or family, now is a good time to do that. It will save you from having to make introductions on the day of your wedding.

Select the date.

Set your budget.

Ask or hire someone to help you organize your thoughts and tasks.

Reserve the wedding and reception sites.

Select a new date since your reception site is already booked for that day.

Start every sentence with "My fiancé and I . . ."

Choose a caterer.

Compile the guest list.

Trim guest list from 758 guests.

Book florist, caterer, cake baker, musicians for the wedding and the reception, photographer, videographer, and limo or other transportation.

Choose your officiant.

Choose your attendants.

Choose your official wedding colors.

Try on gowns.

Vow to lose that extra twenty pounds you've been attempting to lose since birth.

Realize how much money this wedding is really going to cost and reset your budget.

Start considering which songs you want played — and which you want to avoid. Some to pass over: "Love Stinks," "To

All the Girls I've Loved Before," "Send in the Clowns," "I'd Rather Have Jesus."

Schedule to have an engagement portrait taken.

Realize after you've set the date for the portrait, you still have to lose that extra weight. Call back photography studio and reschedule for several months from now.

Have an engagement party.

Schedule for your premarital counseling.

Buy bottle of extra strength aspirin.

Four to Six Months

"Discuss" with your fiancé why his second-grade best friend, BoBo, doesn't need to be invited.

Cut guest list from 523 guests.

Look for bridesmaids' dresses.

Threaten to choose new bridesmaids.

Complete bridal registry.

Order the wedding cake.

Purchase headpiece, jewelry, undergarments, accessories, and personal trousseau.

Schedule a physical exam with your doctor—that includes a Pap smear. And discuss birth control options.

Announce engagement in newspaper.

Order invitations and thank-you cards.

Reserve attire for groom and groomsmen.

"Discuss" with your fiancé why he and the groomsmen cannot wear sneakers to the wedding.

Purchase wedding rings.

Choose favors.

Remind fiancé of his responsibility to plan and book honeymoon.

Decide to "help" fiancé book honeymoon after he announces he's found this great resort for twenty-four bucks a night.

Purchase wedding present for your groom.

Order cake topper, place cards, napkins, matchbooks, cake boxes, favors, toasting glasses, and any other decorations for the wedding or reception.

Make wedding day appointments for hair and makeup.

Provide travel fares and lodging information for out-of-town guests.

Reserve accommodations for out-of-town guests.

Practice saying, "That's an interesting idea. I'll have to discuss that with my fiancé."

Have first of many inane arguments with your fiancé about — well, about inane things.

Two to Four Months

Buy another bottle of extra strength aspirin — but check the sale ads. You're on a budget.

Discover invitations weigh too much.

Go to post office and purchase more postage.

Call half your guest list to get their current addresses.

Begin addressing invitations or hire a calligrapher.

Finalize arrangements with vendors: caterer, baker, florist, musicians, photographer, videographer, and limousine company.

Call fiancé fifteen times every day.

Reserve and plan bridesmaid luncheon: Finalize location, date, time, menu, program, and invitations.

Choose, order, and engrave gifts for attendants.

Notice coworkers and friends begin to complain that your attention span drifts when discussing anything other than wedding details.

Finalize honeymoon plans: Update or request passport, gather tickets, and get inoculations.

Discuss details of the menu with your caterer.

Discuss service with your officiant.

Decide what will happen in your ceremony: readings, special music . . .

Decide whether you will write your vows or will take traditional vows.

Discover you hate the way your fiancé laughs. Wonder if you're marrying the right man.

Schedule your rehearsal time and rehearsal dinner.

Tell your fiancé you are not having the rehearsal meal at Pizza Palace.

One to Two Months

Discover every other sentence you use includes the word *tulle.*

As presents begin to arrive, discover you're receiving two of everything—even of the items for which you never registered.

If your state requires a blood test, have that done.

Buy a guest book.

Finalize ceremony with officiant.

Plan seating chart for reception.

Prep and stuff the invitation envelopes. Include the extra postage.

Mail wedding invitations to arrive six weeks prior to the wedding date.

Address and stamp wedding announcements and arrange for a friend to mail them the day of the wedding.

Send biweekly updates by e-mail or newsletter to wedding party and families.

Have wedding programs printed.

Catch a misspelling in the program—after the printing is done.

Try to prepare your mother-in-law for the misspelled word—her name.

If you decide to change your surname, begin filling out the proper documents.

Send change-of-address information to the post office, magazine subscriptions, banks, workplace, your parents.

Write out place cards.

Mail rehearsal dinner invitations to arrive a few days after the wedding invitations.

If writing own vows, write them.

Discuss financial, business, and legal details: joint bank accounts, wills, change-of-address and name forms. Buy floater insurance to cover gifts.

Decide on a hairstyle and practice it with the headpiece.

Attend first of many bridal showers.

Plaster smile on face during quirky shower games.

Write thank-you notes as you receive presents.

Record and display wedding gifts.

Schedule final fittings for wedding attire.

Sit for formal wedding portrait.

Confirm duties with all wedding helpers: flower pinners, decorators, personal attendants, setup crew, candle lighters, gift and guest table attendants, greeters, seaters, servers, announcers, cake cutters.

Apply and sign for marriage license.

Arrange ceremony and reception parking for wedding party.

Skip writing the thank-yous and decide to do them later.

Receive first RSVP. Realize your wedding is really happening. Squeal with delight.

Become overwhelmed with everything you still have to do.
Give serious thought to eloping.

Two Weeks

Wake in a cold sweat from the nightmare of walking down the aisle naked.

Determine to resume your diet.

Put favors together.

Wonder why you chose to do favors after sticking three hundred handfuls of Jordan almonds in tulle and tying with ribbon.

Choose your "something old, something new, something borrowed, something blue."

Respond to calls from people who have sent gifts and haven't received their thank-you cards yet.

Determine final guest count from RSVP cards received.

Make follow-up phone calls to all guests who never RSVPed.

Finalize seating chart and report final guest count to caterer.

Renotify caterer of new final guest count after fourteen people call to cancel.

Arrange new seating plan — for the seventh time.

Have final dress fitting. Realize you forgot your shoes and run back home.

Assemble and pack items to be taken to the ceremony and reception (wedding programs, favors, decorations, toasting glasses, serving pieces . . .).

Confirm all appointments and arrangements with venues and vendors, including travel reservations.

Notify wedding party of rehearsal time.

Break in wedding shoes at home.

Put together wedding day emergency kit (painkillers, snack bars, breath mints, bottled water, extra hosiery, needle and thread, safety pins, makeup, stain remover).

Deal with family member who threatens not to attend wedding.

Set aside time to have nervous breakdown.

Realize you don't have time or money in budget for a nervous breakdown, so snap out of it.

One Week

Realize you are incapable of making even one more decision.

Ask mother if anyone has ever died from planning a wedding.

Pick up dress or have it delivered.

Pack for honeymoon.

Confirm travel arrangements.

Confirm details with caterer, florist, musicians, officiant, fiancé.

Remind fiancé of time and place of wedding.

Remind best man, BoBo, of time and place of wedding.

Host bridesmaid luncheon.

Have facial or other beauty treatment.

Find your first gray hair (or if you've already been blessed with gray hair, find that your hair is coming out in clumps).

Go to tanning bed.

Figure out which makeup to use to cover your sunburned nose from tanning bed.

One Day before the Wedding

Finalize seating chart—for the eleventh time.

Have manicure and pedicure.

Remind groom to have hair cut and to shave.

Notice you have a permanent deer-caught-in-the-headlights look.

Break down into a fit of hysterical sobs.

Fix your makeup and head for the rehearsal.

Rehearse ceremony.

Lecture ushers and groomsmen that they are not to touch your fiancé's shoes or car or do anything that would otherwise embarrass you on your wedding day, or you will personally break their kneecaps.

Quickly wrap bridal party gifts on way to rehearsal dinner.

Hold rehearsal dinner.

Get eight hours of sleep.

Your Wedding Day

Get up early—even if you haven't slept.

Discover huge pimple or cold sore on face.

Have massage or take hot bubble bath.

Eat hearty breakfast.

Take walk.

Pray and meditate.

Spend a few moments with those special to you.

Have hair and makeup done.

Get to the church on time!

The officiant informs you your groom has arrived—dressed accordingly.

Get married—and have a wonderful day! At least you think you did—you don't remember anything.

Your Wedding Night

Collapse from exhaustion.

No wonder this period in life is considered one of the most stressful times (especially since most brides squeeze many of the above details into the last two weeks). Just reading this list is enough to make you hyperventilate at the sheer enormousness of the wedding planning task.

If that's the place you find yourself, it's time to bring in the big guns. Find someone who will help you focus and organize. This person won't make the decisions for you — or at least, shouldn't! — but will help you know which task to wrestle with when. Amanda, the gal who insisted she didn't experience stress, hired a wedding coordinator and found her to be a tremendous asset. You may want to ask a close friend whom you trust (someone who isn't in your bridal party) to be your coordinator. Or if you and your mother get along, you might consider asking her. If that sends your blood pressure skyrocketing, however, hire the coordinator. If you can't think of anyone, ask a former bride to help or to offer recommendations. After all, she's been there, done that.

And I have some freeing news for you — a secret: *Only two items on that list* have *to be done:* finding an officiant and getting a marriage license. *Everything else is a nonessential.*

— Quick Tips —

Keep a journal and commit to writing in it from the time you get engaged until your wedding day. Otherwise you will forget and become oblivious to everything through your engagement period, and there are sweet, wonderful moments you won't want to forget.

Jeane, married four years

Breathe!

Amy, married five years

— Quick Quips —

Expect something to go wrong at your wedding! There's no other way to say it. A wedding has all the ingredients necessary for a disaster waiting to happen.

H. Norman Wright, marriage and family therapist

A man with pierced ears is better prepared for marriage. He has experienced pain and bought jewelry.

Rita Rudner, comedian

I had the best time just practicing my new signature! I'd write it over and over and wonder, *Should I make the loops in my new last name big or small?*

Karen Campbell, publicist

Two

First Things First

The classic author Charles Dickens best summed up this engagement period in a woman's life: "It was the best of times, it was the worst of times." Sure, people recognize this as the opening line from *A Tale of Two Cities*, but don't be fooled. I'm convinced he stole that line from his wife, who was referring to their engagement period.

Brace yourself for a tumultuous emotional journey from elation to panic to doubt to elation to fear to insanity to elation. Not only do you have the actual work of planning a celebratory soiree known as the wedding and reception, you will also have to deal with many emotional experiences that will arise because of the hoopla. But how do you survive all that *and* keep clear skin and look gorgeous for the big day?

Any wedding preparation book worth its salt will tell you there are a few things you *must* do before you can even begin the "fun" stuff of wading through endless bridesmaid fabric swatches, planning honeymoon destinations, or figuring out which nephew will be the cute, squirmy, nondisruptive ring bearer. The first, of course, is to pick a date. One interesting thing to keep in mind about setting your date is that almost every bride I spoke with mentioned six months is about the ideal amount of time to plan a wedding. Anything longer may cause you to change your mind about wedding details or to second-guess your decisions.

The second thing is to decide how much money you will be able to spend. Unless your father has several seats on the Board of Trade and is able to drop $100,000 on a wedding, you're probably going to need to set a budget.

Budget Blowout

According to *Ladies' Home Journal* the average wedding costs nearly $22,360.[1] So with good reason every book or magazine you read is going to rant about the importance of setting a budget. While I agree wholeheartedly with budget planning, I found setting a realistic one to be a bit more idealistic. I really had no idea how much everything would cost. I set aside a certain amount of money for the caterer; then I met with the caterer and realized I was off on my calculations. Then I ended up going back to my budget and erasing and refiguring.

You need to assess how much money you can afford to spend — sans the credit cards. If you plan to pay for everything, which I recommend (I'll discuss the reasons later), then you'll know pretty quickly what your budget should be. If, for instance, you have a savings account with $125 in it, then you've either set your wedding date for twelve years from now or you plan to take a second job. In my case, when Scott and I started to date seriously, I began slamming every penny into my savings account, and I took on some freelance work to supplement my income.

31

Once you calculate the total you're able to spend, break that down into amounts you will spend for flowers, cake, musicians, wedding officiant, dress, and whatever else you must buy. This is where I found the wedding books lacking. I had never been married before; how was I supposed to know how much to budget? If I budgeted $500 for flowers, would I end up with carnations and baby's breath and that would be all?

Next, try to prioritize what is most important to you. I knew which reception hall I absolutely wanted and didn't care how much it would cost. Therefore I planned to spend more money on that than on decorations. But if you've always wanted tulips imported from Holland, you'll want to make sure you set more aside for that expense. One former coworker told me she was pretty conservative on her wedding except for one frivolous expenditure: She had the florist and his team hand-open each long-stem rose at each reception table. During the cocktail hour, her florist was busily blossoming almost one thousand roses. I shiver to think of the expense of that one!

One tip: Your reception will be the area in which you will experience the most monetary surprises. This is the area in your budget you will need to revisit every day until the day after the wedding, so be sure you write your budget in pencil and carry a large eraser with you at all times.

After you set your budget, tape a big note on your car's dashboard that reads: "Our budget is set; weddings are a billion-dollar industry; salespeople will attempt to make me spend more money than the gross national product of Argentina; it's okay to say no." (A sign that just reads "It's okay to say no" would work too.) Then practice smiling while saying these words: *"No, thank you."* This is important. Those words will be your lifeline to preserve you from entering your marriage with a titanic-sized debt. Salespeople in this industry are ruthless and cunning. They'll act overly interested in you, your life, and your wedding. Do not be deceived; they'll only remember you as long as it takes for your check to clear the bank.

Who Will Pay?

If you are a student planning a wedding, you will probably need some financial aid from your folks or some other generous donor to help you defray the costs. However, if you have gainful employment, I recommend you pay for your own wedding. That way, you can enjoy guilt-free spending.

One reason I wanted to pay for my wedding was because I wanted that to be a present to my parents. They reared me, helped pay for college, got me settled into my first apartment, and provided a down payment for a car.

If your fiancé is going to help pay for the wedding, you two need to sit down and decide the amount you are willing to spend. This is a good time to discuss your finances anyway, since you may combine them once you're married.

If someone else plans to help pay for your wedding — a parent, grandparent, benevolent stranger, long-lost relative — you and your fiancé will definitely need to sit down with that person or persons immediately to discuss how much they're willing to spend.

This is important because you want to be aware of what they can afford. Try to be sensitive to their budget. Usually parents want what's best for their children — even if they can't afford it. Take that into consideration when they offer their finances. If they insist on paying even though you planned to pay, compromise by allowing them to provide for something specific. That way you can still honor them. For instance, my parents paid for our hotel room on our wedding night. Another bride's parents were thrilled to pay for the honeymoon.

One caveat to having other people pay for your wedding: Those who help you may expect to have some control over your wedding choices. Leslie found this to be true. Her in-laws-to-be offered to help financially — and offered their own ideas for wedding planning. "That was a difficult position to be in," says Leslie. "Since they were paying for it, Bill and I spent a lot of evenings listening to what they wanted our wedding to be."

Special Splurges

You may want to splurge in some special areas. While you probably should not do this in every area, I think at least one splurge is okay—as long as you can afford it. Scott and I splurged on a horse-drawn carriage to drive us to the reception. Another bride, Jennifer, splurged on a nicer dress. Just try not to splurge so much that you need to take out a loan.

Don't forget to add in pampering costs to your budget. You may want to pamper yourself with things like a manicure, pedicure, facial, massage, special perfume, tanning salons, and honeymoon lingerie.

Usually there will be other areas in which you will be able to cut costs to afford those special extras. Cut, cut away. However, you definitely will not want to cut in certain areas. One of those is the photographer. As the saying goes, "You get what you pay for" (we'll discuss this more on p. 70). If you ask your friend who's an amateur photographer and who owns a "one step" camera with a red-eye detector to be your photographer, trust me, you'll probably get few—if any—photos you'll want to hang over your fireplace mantel. There may be some you'll want to hang *in* the fireplace, however.

Words of Caution

Credit cards are tempting. Just be careful using them, or they might eat up the joy from your marriage when, after the honeymoon, those bills show up—and you still can't pay them. Do yourself a favor, do your marriage a favor, do anyone else a favor who's helping to cover the wedding costs—don't go into debt, and don't allow anyone else to either.

One bride, Jeane, told me, "We had our wedding in October and we were conscious not to see the wedding in November." In other words, pay only what you can afford. Don't start your marriage in debt.

On the other hand, if you choose to use credit cards, you can use them to your advantage. I used my card because it had a cash back deal. I paid off the balance each month with the cash from my wedding savings account and ended up with a nice, fat rebate check that Scott and I used to pay for a romantic weekend after we were married.

Another point to mention is check the fine print on your contracts. I put my down payment for the reception hall on my credit card. The banquet coordinator failed to point out that they add 3 percent to all credit card payments. Not until after I had already paid using that method did I read that juicy little tidbit. You are already forking out a hefty chunk of change — why give them the extra when you don't have to? For a $300 payment, that ends up being $9. While $9 doesn't seem like a lot, it adds up. And every penny counts when you are planning a wedding.

Making the Cut

After you have determined your budget, you will want to decide the type and size of the wedding. Ideally, you are probably considering inviting everyone you have ever met. My mother was so excited about the engagement, she threatened to rent a billboard on I-77 announcing: "My daughter's getting married! Everyone invited."

Lisa and Bryan had a year to plan their wedding. They'd been out of school about a year, so finances were tight. Lisa wanted a small wedding — something in their budget, but that would be special and memorable. The snag came as they began to compile their guest list. Just counting family members, the list soared to more than one hundred guests — not the small wedding Lisa had ideally wanted. And that list didn't include their friends. "We didn't know what to do," Lisa says. "Bryan and I wanted something small, yet we felt we had to invite our family and friends. But that made it large!" With each month that passed, Lisa and Bryan vacillated between having a large or a smaller, more intimate wedding. Finally, as they watched the guest list continue to grow and knew they couldn't afford the size, they decided that the ones they really needed to please were not their family and friends, but each other. That's when they decided to go out of town to a small tourist area several hours from their home to have their ceremony and spend their honeymoon. They would invite only immediate family and their closest friends, which ended up being about twenty-five people total. "We informed everyone of our plans and told them they were welcome to attend," Lisa says. "But we knew most wouldn't make the long drive, which definitely helped our budget."

Let's face it, choosing your guest list is one of the most difficult decisions you may ever make. How do you invite three hundred of your most intimate family, friends, and coworkers, as well as the extra hundred intimate friends, coworkers, and business associates of your parents and your future in-laws, not to mention all those people you were close to a decade ago who invited you to their wedding? Martha Williamson writes in her book *Inviting God to Your Wedding*, "There is perhaps no other occasion that occurs in life when you are called upon to make a list of everyone you know and care about and then essentially rank them in importance. It is a harsh truth to realize that this is what you're finally doing when you create your guest list."[2]

Amelia and Tim decided they would have one hundred and fifty people at their wedding, with each of them choosing seventy-five people. But Amelia's mom decided that wasn't enough. So she ordered her own invitations (four hundred of them) and mailed them. "To this day," says Amelia, "I have no idea how many invitations my mother actually sent. But the church was packed, and we had two receptions—one with just cake and punch and the other a more intimate get together for our close family and friends. That was a pain—but we received a lot of wedding presents!"

If you are having difficulty over the guest list, consider this: Some statistics say that about 25 percent of the people you invite won't attend. If you invite one hundred guests, more than likely only about seventy-five will show up. So if your mother-in-law is adamant about inviting her beautician and the postman and her childhood friend from Arizona, who probably won't attend anyway, why not honor her and invite them?

If your father is deadset on inviting business associates he sees once a year and who have never met you, you have a decision to make. Is the present they give you going to be worth it? And are they worth the $125 it's going to cost to feed them? Just kidding.

The thing to remember is that you and your groom have the final say—unless someone else is helping to pay for the wedding. If that's the case (see the section on budgeting earlier), you'll need to compromise. *Then* think about how nice the wedding present will hopefully be. Maybe they'll give you cash . . .

Tricky Guest Dilemmas

Now is the time to decide if you want to have a child-free wedding. This needs to be something you and your fiancé agree on so you can present a united front. If you agree to allow children, know that the elegance level of your wedding is going to go down a notch. I realize that's probably an un-PC thing to say, but elegance just "ain't gonna happen." You'll want to make sure you have kid-friendly activities for the ceremony. While you would think most parents would bring crayons and toys, they won't. And if your ceremony is long, those children will act like, well, children. They'll get fidgety, which means they'll get loud, which means they'll disrupt and make it difficult for the guests sitting in their vicinity to enjoy the ceremony. As an option, you might want to consider hiring a baby-sitter for the ceremony itself.

The same goes for the reception. If you want to serve lobster bisque, you probably aren't planning for children to be present. Think through your options and make sure to inquire if the caterer can provide child-friendly foods.

However, if you and your fiancé have children, you will definitely want to include them, regardless of whether or not other children are invited. Not only are you joining together as a couple, you're joining together as a ready-made family. And it's only natural for your brood to experience some insecurity as to how important they will be to the family. This is a great opportunity to include them in the ceremony, to let them know how special and meaningful they are to both you and your fiancé.

Another dilemma is what to do about divorced guests — especially if they are part of your family or the groom's. Eileen was thrilled about her engagement to Lee and wanted to show her appreciation to Lydia, the woman who had played matchmaker to them. The problem was that Lydia was Lee's recently divorced sister-in-law, and Lee's brother was one of the groomsmen — and was engaged to another woman. Eileen was in a quandary. "I really wanted her there — or at least wanted to invite her — to thank her for bringing Lee into my life," Eileen says. "But after Lee and I discussed it, we decided not to send her an invitation because it would cause too much pain and discomfort to Lee's brother and his fiancé. Instead, I decided to write her a thank-you note to express how grateful I was for her keen insight into what I needed in my life."

Divorce has torn asunder many brides' hopes for a wonderful, joy-filled wedding day. Feuds and just plain immature people have also had a field day with a bride's nerves. If you face this dilemma, there is hope. Here are several items to consider: Don't allow yourself to be blackmailed or manipulated. Keep everyone's feelings in mind, but the final choice is up to you. Carrie's fiancé's parents were divorced, and the newlyweds-to-be were trying to decide how to keep the peace and invite his mother as well as his new stepmom to a family gathering the morning of the wedding. They decided to honor both with an invitation. "We decided if they became upset," says Carrie, "that was their problem."

If anyone threatens not to attend if you invite the questionable person, then recognize they aren't honoring you on your most important day. Let them know you'd love for them to share in the celebration, but it's their choice if they choose not to attend. Don't allow them to put their blame on you, because you won't kowtow to such schemes.

In her book *Inviting God to Your Wedding*, Martha Williamson gives some great tips for trying to decide whom to include on your guest list:

1. Don't invite anyone out of obligation.
2. Ask God for wisdom and guidance.
3. Only invite those people who will genuinely share your joy on that day.

Martha adds,

Think twice before inviting anyone you can reasonably predict will bring only "negative vibes." That holds true even if the potential toxic guest is your uncle or your godmother or your mother's best friend or your father's business associate. This is your day, and even though you want to be a good hostess, this is not the day for you to bear the burden of family problems or old enmities or simply people with bad attitudes who should know better.[3]

Having Your Fiancé Help

There's a scene in the hit sitcom *Everybody Loves Raymond* in which the lead character, Ray Romano, and his wife, Deborah, take a walk down memory lane to the time when they became engaged and began planning their wedding. The following scene ensues:

Ray proposes to Deborah, who says yes, then immediately wants to show him her plans for the wedding.

"Plans?" Ray says.

"Yes," says Deborah. "I've been planning this since I was twelve."

"But you didn't meet me 'til you were twenty-two."

"You're the last piece of the puzzle," Deborah replies.

Then Deborah whips out her "plans," which include releasing doves after the ceremony, as Ray looks on confused and a bit dismayed.

The next scene takes place with Deborah and her parents discussing the details, leaving Ray standing nearby, looking on motionless and mute. Finally, Ray summons the nerve to say, "I'm invited, right?"

I don't know who wrote that episode, but they nailed the truth. Many of us brides have planned most of the details since we were twelve years old, and our fiancé is the last piece of the puzzle—although we'd never admit that.

Many books will recommend that you have your fiancé help plan the wedding. Lisa's fiancé, Steve, planned the entire event. That was one of his gifts—he was creative and wanted to give her a special day. Ann's fiancé, Mark, was also creatively gifted and wanted to be part of the planning process—although Mark will be the first to admit, "Ann probably wasn't all that thrilled that I had as many opinions as I did."

Amy was surprised by how important certain things were to her fiancé, Trei. "He was very opinionated about picking the correct sterling silverware pattern. Who would have thought that would be so important to him?" she says.

I had just finished reading Martha Williamson's book *Inviting God to Your Wedding,* in which she suggested having your fiancé participate. So I talked to Scott and told him I wanted him to be part of the planning. He told me he appreciated my offer and he'd love to be involved.

Silly me. I figured he meant he'd love to go with me and say, "Yes, sweetie, I like that color too," or, "I completely agree with your cake choice." In other words, I wanted his opinion as long as it was my opinion spoken in his voice. Boy, was I surprised when he started to share his ideas and they were different than mine. I realized I was expecting him to want to do things my way, but that we'd do them *together* my way.

The most painful example was one evening at the mall. Over dinner we were discussing the reception, and Scott said he hated announcing the wedding party and thought we shouldn't do that. I, on the other hand, definitely wanted to do that. Nothing would change his mind. "It's silly," he said.

Frustrated, I said finally, "Well, then, what do you suggest?"

"Let's do nothing."

My look of disbelief must have made him concoct a Plan B, because then he added, "Or we could already be at the head table and stand when the deejay announces everyone."

I could just envision the bridesmaids and me pushing back our chairs, wiggling to get out of our seats, *gracefully*, and knocking over the candelabras.

"No, absolutely not," I said. "You haven't seen my dress, but trust me, that's not going to work. I wouldn't be able to get up and down for an introduction, plus it would look ridiculous." End of discussion, or so I thought. We stewed over this predicament and carried it right out into the mall on the way to the tuxedo store. I don't remember much of our argument as we walked past the shops, but I do remember us throwing out words such as *childish*, *spoiling*, *my*, and *never*. These are probably not the best things to be shouting at your beloved in the middle of a mall. But there we were. Scott walked away, leaving me standing alone by the Gap, as I shouted, "You are *so* immature." Obviously not one of my finer moments.

I think our situation would have been different had I informed Scott upfront that I wanted his input and wanted him to be involved, but that I also had certain expectations of how

I wanted the wedding—and those were ideas I'd been noodling for years.

Here's the truth: Many of us have been planning our big day since as long as we can remember. Our men, on the other hand, have been planning it since they decided to buy the ring—and some of them not even then. We exceed them in the planning/expectation department by about 150 percent. So to be fair we need to let them know, honestly but gently, that we have certain desires. That doesn't mean we can't change our desires or be flexible, but it may take us a while to get our head around the fact that we're going to make a change. And while we also know there are hundreds of wonderful qualities about our betrothed, wedding planning just may not be one of his talents.

My suggestion is to do what feels comfortable for you—while still honoring your husband-to-be. After all, if it weren't for him, you wouldn't be planning your nuptials. While you will be the focus, your man is still a nonnegotiable to the entire wedding. Make this an opportunity to exercise your communication and compromise skills. Take an evening before you start planning everything and present your thoughts and expectations for the wedding and honeymoon.

My friend Karen got married last year. She's Dutch. The man she married is Scottish—as in, bagpipers played and the men wore kilts. This was not originally what she had in mind for her wedding. But she allowed herself to be flexible and to expand her wish list, and she thought it might be cool to have something unique. So while she originally envisioned a traditional ceremony with some Dutch elements woven throughout, she compromised and was pleasantly pleased with a traditional Scottish wedding with Dutch elements woven throughout. Her lesson? "Be willing to compromise and talk through every-thing," she says.

Some fiancés won't care to help on all the details. Amy and her fiancé, Todd, got into a doozy of an argument when she asked for his opinion on something about the ceremony. His response was, "I don't care, do whatever you want." Wrong thing to say. "I burst into tears and yelled, 'You don't care about this wedding!'" says Amy. "But that wasn't true. He did care about the wedding; he just didn't care about all the details. And I was so stressed, his response set me off."

Deep down your fiancé does care about your wedding. He just may be shell-shocked and feeling overwhelmed too. Or he may feel overloaded with all the details and information. Does he care what color the flowers are? Maybe not. Does he care if you show up? I'd say bank on it. Ask him how much he wants to be informed. If it's a major development — say your reception hall burned to the ground and you need to find another place — you'd probably want to tell him about that. It may also be a good idea to let him know the day and time of the actual ceremony.

Wedding Mission

Before you begin to plan your wedding, it may be worthwhile to discuss what your wedding priorities are with your fiancé. Anna and her fiancé, John, discussed this right after their engagement. They decided they wanted a God-centered wedding, and their top priorities were to have good music and the right people in attendance. This became a lifesaver when they encountered opposition from outside sources.

When Anna's mom wanted to invite people whom Anna didn't want to attend, she remembered her mission statement and those priorities, one of which was to have the right people. That made it easier for Anna to explain to her mother the importance of sticking to the original plans and easier to say no to her mother's demands.

"John and I just kept going back to those priorities," says Anna. "If something didn't fit into those, we were able to say no and feel strong about that decision. I didn't feel as though I had to justify what I wanted for my own wedding."

Regardless of what your mission statement is (it can be as straightforward as one bride's: simple, sacred, and elegant), you and your fiancé will want to talk about it so you are both on the same page. That will alleviate some of the stress in your planning.

— Quick Tips —

Be ready for uninvited people to be upset because they weren't invited (especially with smaller weddings). They'll get over it—and if they don't, you were right in not inviting them.

Leslie, married three years

It's okay to say no.

Angel, married two years

THREE

A Family Affair

When Amelia became engaged she phoned her mother, who lived across the country. Her mother wanted her to fly home to shop for her gown. Amelia explained that she was going to look for her dress locally, and her mom replied coldly, "Well, don't get it in white. You don't look good in white."

"I'm not getting white. I'm going with off-white," Amelia said.

Her mother said, "You don't look good in off-white either."

After Amelia hung up the phone, she cried. "Her comments were so cutting," says Amelia. "I became angry with her. But later Mom confessed she wished she could have been there to help me pick out my dress. That's when I realized she hadn't meant to be hurtful. She was speaking from her own frustration that she wasn't there. She felt left out."

Many times when someone is unable to express their pain, they use insensitive words. That was Amelia's mom's way of coping. Was it the right way? No. But when Amelia understood why her mother said what she did, it was easier to brush off the remarks and not allow them to offend her any longer.

Sometimes, however, family members will say or do something incredibly hurtful apparently out of spite. That happened to Ruth on her wedding day. Her future stepmother-in-law refused to attend the wedding, then called the reception hall, demanded to speak with Ruth's new husband, and yelled at him for not inviting her. "She really gave him an earful," says Ruth. "My husband apologized that she never received her invitation, but we knew we sent her one. She was just a spiteful woman." Fortunately, Ruth had learned to pay little attention to those malicious outbursts. "When she first started making insensitive comments," Ruth says, "I was offended, but I eventually realized I wasn't the problem, she was. For whatever reason, she was a deeply unhappy person. I stopped taking her comments personally. The next time she said something, I looked at her and thought, *Well, consider the source*. That helped me let her comments go in one ear and out the other."

The Forgiveness Factor

One of the things I love about a wedding is that it's a chance to start something fresh. The old has passed, the new has come. And part of starting anew is to let go of some things from the past, to make peace.

Anna knew the importance of going into her marriage "clean." She wanted to heal her estranged relationship with her mother before she got married. "I wanted everything to be a clean slate," she says. So she and her mother had a long talk in which both women communicated their feelings and offered forgiveness. "It was a great first step to healing," says Anna. "And there wasn't a blot on my life going into my marriage."

Author Alan Paton, who wrote *Cry, the Beloved Country,* explains why we should take the first step to forgive: "There is a hard law. . . . When an injury is done to us, we never recover until we forgive."

Choosing to forgive. It's not an easy thing sometimes. But if we don't forgive, we cannot fully move into the future. And the longer we harbor unforgiveness, the more it turns into bitterness.

Why is this important at this point? Because no longer are you single. Your injuries become your spouse's and vice versa. They affect your marriage — maybe not in tangible ways, but they do affect it.

So how do you forgive? Many times we get the idea that it's a one-time deal. Anna found that her conversation with her mother was just the tip of the proverbial iceberg. "I offered my forgiveness," Anna says, "but every time bitter thoughts arose I had to forgive her again."

Depending on the nature of the hurt, you may have to keep forgiving over and over. Jesus talked about forgiving someone seventy times seven times (Matt. 18:22). The best way to do it is to ask God to help you forgive. Also, talk to a trusted friend or counselor who can help you let go. The more you do, the easier it becomes.

Mother, May I . . .

Planning a wedding can bring you and your mother closer as you bond over choosing flowers and wedding gowns. It can also be the worst time of your life. You may entertain visions of wrapping an entire roll of duct tape around your mom's mouth — especially after the fiftieth time she says, "Well, if it were me . . ." or "If I were you . . ."

When I was discussing this book with my friend Amanda, she said, "Tell them to watch out for their mothers. She'll bulldoze right over you to plan your wedding." Amanda's mom didn't even bother with the phrase, "If I were you." She just went ahead and took charge. For instance, Amanda and her fiancé wanted a low-key, informal barbeque reception. But to her dismay, she ended up with a second reception directly following the ceremony—something her mother had planned. "I admit," says Amanda, "in the end, I'm glad she helped out as much as she did because I couldn't have done everything. But it was definitely a bumpy road for us!"

While your mother may have a knack for finding your last nerve and tap dancing all over it, there is one thing you may want to keep in mind. When you started planning your wedding at the age of twelve, your mom was more than likely also planning your wedding and building her own expectations about your special day. After all, she's considered the official hostess of the wedding day. To her, the success of your day reflects on her as well. It's almost as if she's getting married again. Her friends celebrate her daughter's wedding day with her. It's a joyous occasion in her life as well as in yours.

Your mother wants your wedding to be a success because then she's a success. She wants things to be perfect—just as you do. The problem comes when her idea of perfection veers away from your idea of perfection.

What should you do when that happens? You can take a deep breath and try to see things from her point of view. Why is she doing or saying certain things that bother you?

One bride, Mary, had always had a tense relationship with her mother. She tried to clear the air. They met, hashed out some issues, and forgave each other. As they turned over a new leaf, they began to call each other more during the week to try to create a mother-daughter connection that hadn't been there previously. When Mary became engaged, her mother was thrilled and said, "Oh, this is the perfect time for us to bond."

Instead, Mary felt as if her mother were trying to control everything. "She was trying to pick out my dress, tell me when to register, and choose my style of reception. She was making me insane!" says Mary. "Now that I look back, though, I think Mom saw it as an opportunity for us to draw closer. She just didn't know how to do it that well—and neither did I." What

Mary did do, though, was to make sure she kept her mom abreast of her plans. When she found her wedding dress, she made sure her mom saw it right away. "My mom can be very dominating. She has a good heart, but she's dominating," says Mary. "I had to communicate with her that I appreciated her interest in my affairs, but that I was the one making the final decision."

The Bible talks about how to handle your mother. As a matter of fact, it's one of the top Ten Commandments from God: "Honor your father and mother." Unfortunately, it doesn't say, "Honor your father and your mother — except when they drive you crazy." Go figure. However, the Bible offers a reward if you honor your parents: "Then you will live a long, full life in the land the LORD your God will give you" (Exod. 20:12).

Honoring your mom doesn't mean you have to do everything she requests. It's not really about making her happy, it's about building a relationship with her.

It means out of respect for her position, you listen and hear her out and consider her request. Even if you choose not to agree with her opinions or take her advice, at least allow her to voice them. You can still honor her as well by communicating clearly your expectations and boundaries: "Mom, I appreciate everything you're doing for me by helping me plan my wedding. I understand this is an important day for you too. I will give your comments careful consideration, but if I don't follow them, I need you to understand it's not because they're not worthy of being heard. It's just that I have certain expectations too."

Then breathe again. Regardless of the type of mother you have, you can still make this time an enjoyable bonding experience. But that comes with sharing honestly your thoughts, feelings, and desires.

When Parents Grieve

I was on my way home from work when my father called me on the cell phone. He sounded depressed.

"Hey, Dad! How are you?" I said.

He was quiet for a moment, then he said "Hi, Chip" (his nickname for me). "I was just driving home from a meeting and heard Elvis on the radio singing 'I Can't Help Falling in Love with You'" (Scott's and my "song" we would be dancing to at the reception). "I started to tear up."

My father was grieving his loss.

There's a saying, "You're not losing a daughter, you're gaining a son-in-law." Depending on the son-in-law, some fathers have a right to cry! (Not over *your* fiancé, of course.) But that old saying simply isn't true. Your parents *are* losing a daughter. From your wedding day on, your relationship with your parents will never be the same.

My mom would say, "You won't be completely mine anymore." And I'd reassure her it wasn't true; I wouldn't change. But I did.

Parents can be pretty smart.

But the change is supposed to happen! You no longer belong to your family. You belong to your husband, as Jesus said: "A man leaves his father and mother and is joined to his wife, and the two are united into one. Since they are no longer two but one, let no one separate them, for God has joined them together" (Matt. 19:5–6).

Your parents know the truth of that statement. While they are thrilled for you because they want you to be happy, they also know you will break from them and join with your spouse. No longer will you go to them first. Nor should you.

There may be occasions during your engagement when your mom or dad will withdraw or become depressed, or they may become irritable. Instead of reacting in frustration, take a moment to consider that they may be hurting because they know in some way your relationship will change after your wedding.

When you notice those times, it can become an opportunity for you to extend grace to them. Send them a quick note or a card that reassures them you love them, that you remember them, and that your love won't change.

Mothers-in-law are also pretty smart. They also realize they are losing their "baby," that son whom they love and care for, for whom they changed so many diapers. This can be a time of great pain for them because they are also mourning the loss of something they will never have again. This isn't a bad thing; it's just a painful thing. Take this time to extend grace to your mother-in-law-to-be.

You may think, *Wait a minute. Why do I have to be the one to extend grace? She's older than me—she should know better!* I remember a conversation I had once with author Stormie Omartian, who told me, "God chooses to work in the one who's the most flexible, the one who is willing to be molded. Why not let him start with you?" Once we extend grace, God will extend grace to us. Jesus talked about doing God-honoring things, even when no one knows about them except you: "God sees what you do in private and will honor (reward) you for doing right" (Matt. 6:4, my paraphrase). Sometimes kindness is difficult to extend, but it's always worth the effort.

When In-Laws Turn Bad

When Jennifer and Troy became engaged, his mother was upset. "She made no secret of the fact that I was not her choice for a daughter-in-law," says Jennifer. "She didn't come to my bridal showers, and she refused to get together with my mother to discuss the wedding." But the clincher came two weeks before the wedding. Every Sunday, Jennifer and Troy went to his parents' house for dinner. However, that Sunday his mother didn't set a place for her at the table. Troy assumed she just forgot. Yet when during the week of the wedding his mother neglected again to set a place for her, Jennifer knew it was intentional. "Imagine the statement she was making," says Jennifer. "If you really think about the implication of not setting a place for you, that's deep," Jennifer says. "That's big."

Before you are married, you are in a precarious position with your future in-laws. At this point, they're not your family. You're still trying to make a good impression, and you tend to overlook or allow a lot of things for the sake of that.

"Troy talked to his dad about that incident," says Jennifer. "But I was crushed. I never really had a good relationship with my mother, and I always dreamed my mother-in-law would fill that void. It was obvious she wasn't interested."

Jennifer learned a difficult lesson that day: "I was not going to allow my future mother-in-law to destroy my happiness. I decided right then to see her through the lens of who she really is. For some people, that's the most they have to give."

Hopefully, you won't have an experience like Jennifer's. One thing to remember is that just as you may be experiencing insecurity as you try to figure out how you belong in his family, the family may be experiencing the same insecurity about how to include you. They've never had you as a daughter-in-law. They love their son; they want what's best for him just as you do. Everyone's forging a new path, and it will get bumpy along the way.

It's important that you realize you need to be careful when criticizing your fiancé's family. (Read: *Don't.*) If your mother-in-law has hinted at setting your wedding cake aflame during the reception, then by all means inform your fiancé of the situation. But stick to the facts and don't stray over into the land of your feelings — if you want to start an argument with Loverboy, that's the way to do it.

You may comment, "By the way, your mother mentioned she was going to set the cake on fire. I'm not sure how to solve this situation. Any thoughts?" If he responds, great. If not, don't take it personally. He may feel you're asking him to take sides, which may be difficult when the sides are the two most important women in his life.

One thing that can help is to stay focused on your fiancé. Jennifer was sure she and Troy were meant to be together. "I knew we were following God," says Jennifer. "We were doing what we were supposed to be doing—even if my mother-in-law didn't like it. I didn't have the attitude, *No one's going to stop us.* It was more an attitude of, *This is so beyond her. This doesn't have anything to do with her.*"

The best thing to do in those situations is to tell yourself, *I'm not going to take this personally. I don't know what's going on within her or why she chooses to say and do those things. But I will not allow it to affect my joy.*

—Quick Tips—

Write out this Scripture verse on a 3x5 card and keep it with you: "A gentle answer turns away wrath, but harsh words stir up anger" (Prov. 15:1). It did wonders during tense moments!

Madelyn, married two years

During the engagement, I don't think you realize what a huge part your in-laws are going to play in your life *forever.* So look for and work on ways to build a bridge in your relationship with them. Include them in as many things as you can, such as planning showers or asking advice on registering. Usually, this will help your relationship get off to a good start.

Amanda, married four years

Now is a good time to accept that his family is different than yours. And will always be different. My husband's family is perfectly fine, but I always make it seem as if my family is ideal and his isn't.

Lisa, married four years

FOUR

Friends, Face-offs, and Free Advice

The Friendship Factor

Julie was thrilled when her boyfriend, Ray, finally proposed to her. Of course, she wanted to share her great news with her best friend, Sally. Julie called Sally, and they decided to meet for lunch.

"I've got something exciting to tell you," Julie started. "Ray and I are getting married!"

Julie held up her hand to show Sally the ring. What she expected to hear from Sally was some sort of congratulations and plenty of "oohs" and "aahs."

What Julie got: a blank stare, silence, then tears. Then, "I can't believe you're getting married. Everyone's getting married except me. This is awful! When will it be my turn?"

54

Julie was crushed. "The one person I expected to be the most excited for me ended up being the one person with whom I couldn't share my life."

Eileen can relate. Upon finding out Eileen was engaged, one of her coworkers informed her, "You really suck right now. You just really . . . suck." It didn't help matters when her coworker found out the wedding was scheduled for the same week as a work-related trip she was supposed to take. "You knew I was taking this trip," Eileen's coworker said. "Yet you still planned your wedding for that weekend."

Eileen was hurt more than anything. "I'm sorry," she told her coworker. "I didn't intentionally sit down with my calendar and try to find the one weekend when you'd be the most inconvenienced."

You may discover your friends will greet your news with varying degrees of enthusiasm. Of course, not all your friends will be self-centered in their response to your announcement. Most of your friends will shower you with whoops and sighs and praises and shrieks of delight. They'll want to live vicariously through your enchanted new life and share in the planning — or at least hear all about it.

But once you place that ring on your finger, you will be quickly thrown into situations in which you'll learn who are the friends you can count on — and who are the women you need to steer clear of during this period, or at least edit your wedding detail information around.

I had a friend, Shawna, who congratulated me but became quiet and withdrawn whenever I would discuss the wedding. She never asked about my plans, nor did she express any interest when others would inquire. I knew she was unhappy being single, and I assumed my nearly-wedded state was magnifying her un-nearly-wedded state. I still spent time with her, but I was so guarded and conscious of everything I said, making sure I didn't mention Scott or the wedding, that it drained my already dwindling supply of energy. I made a conscious choice to limit the time I spent with her. That was difficult, I admit, because I really like Shawna. But I was no longer able to be myself, and I felt as if I were hurting her in some way. I certainly didn't want to "flaunt" my engagement, so I chose to spend time with the friends I could be myself around. I am still friends with Shawna, and she drove nine hours to be at my wedding. But looking back on it, I should have had a heart-to-heart talk with her. I should have explained that I was sensing a change in her and asked if we could talk about it. I think that would have made a difference.

Emma was a bride with a similar problem, except that her unhappily single friend was her maid of honor. "She made it clear she was unhappy that I was getting married and she was not," says Emma. "She was difficult throughout the entire engagement, from refusing to try on bridesmaid dresses to not including the other bridesmaids in shower details. To be honest, I wish she hadn't been my maid of honor."

You may find that some of your single friends will take your engagement as a personal affront to their marital status. Really, it has nothing to do with you, but it *will* affect you. I know this personally because I used to be one of the fair-weather friends. When my friend Amy became engaged, I was unable to be happy for her. I was so self-absorbed about what that meant for me: I was "losing" my best friend and my roommate, and I was going to be second place to her fiancé. I'm ashamed to admit that I rarely asked about her wedding plans, I didn't go dress shopping with her, and I didn't help her with any of the details. I was awful. I can't believe she kept talking to me, frankly. And I was her maid of honor! Yet she was so gracious about it. Even though my attitude was really more about me, it affected her. The one person she should have been able to rejoice with, she couldn't. Although I finally snapped out of it and threw her a bridal shower and helped her the last few days leading up to the wedding, I lost so many opportunities to share in her joy. After I became engaged, I called her and apologized because I realized how immaturely I had acted and how much that must have hurt her.

I learned the hard way, and I lost out because I didn't communicate honestly with Amy or with Shawna. I should have expressed what I was feeling and tried to work through those emotions.

You can never reclaim the days of your engagement. Talk to your friends if you sense a change and ask them to tell you honestly if they sense a change in you! If, after your chat, nothing has altered their attitudes or behavior, then limit your time with them.

Another friend of mine, Diana, was in a difficult marriage when I got engaged. While she asked how Scott proposed to me, it was obvious she was simply being polite. When another friend who hadn't heard me tell the proposal story asked about it, Diana replied, "Yes, Ginger, tell us again the story about your *breathtaking* news." Wow. I picked up her not-so-subtle message—and I didn't elaborate on my story, but rather just told the basics—rather self-consciously at that. Later I overheard her make the comment: "I wish her luck. She's going to need it."

I was crushed. *Why can't she be excited for me?* I wondered. *She's supposed to be my friend.* It wasn't until a few months later, when I heard she was getting a divorce, that the truth of her situation dawned on me. I had taken her harsh words personally, but they weren't meant that way. She was speaking from her own pain.

Some of your friends will probably make insensitive comments to you that may cause you pain. If at all possible, look at what's going on within those friends that might have made them say those things. Try not to take their words personally. You'll be happier if you don't.

"Expert" Advice

You'll be amazed at how many people know so much about what you want or the right thing for you to do. Author Peter F.

Cullip shares this truthful nugget: "The trouble with most sound advice is that it's 99 percent sound and 1 percent advice."[1] You can accept advice graciously—and not allow it to interfere with anything you intended to do in the first place.

But *how* do you accept their "wisdom" gracefully? Here are a few responses that worked for me:

"That's an interesting idea. I'll have to consider that."

"Wow, I never thought of it that way. I'll have to consider that."

And my personal favorite: "Thanks for sharing that idea. I'll have to talk it over with my fiancé."

That last one is what I call the "blame my fiancé" game. One of the things I love about Scott, even to this day, is that he has no problem saying no. He has that boundary thing down. And he doesn't mind being the "bad" guy. I discovered this treasure when someone gave me a "you must do this for your wedding" gem. I thanked her and told her I'd discuss it with Scott. The next time I saw her, she asked, "Are you going to do what I suggested?" I was able to respond, "Oh, Scott and I discussed that, and it's just not good for us. But I appreciate your thoughtfulness in sharing your idea."

Rarely will they push it further, but if they do, stick to your guns. There's no need to defend your choice. Keep mentally going back to your motto: "It's our wedding." Smiling and nodding a lot goes a long way.

Amanda and Tony had a similar situation arise when they chose to get married in March—in Kansas. Not exactly the most picturesque place in March, but they were happy with the date. "But we got so many people questioning our choice of the wedding date," Amanda says. "They kept trying to get us to move the wedding to a different month. I couldn't understand why it mattered so much to them. We were happy with our choice. Why did they care? The wedding wasn't about them!"

Here's the truth: The individuals who pass out advice like candy really don't care. They may gripe about you not following their expertise, but in the end your wedding day will come and go, and they will forget about it. In five years when you look back on your wedding day, you will remember what you wish you had done, what was perfect, and what you hated. And if you follow advice you didn't want, you will have regrets — but the people who passed out all that advice won't even remember. Trust me on this one.

Choosing Bridesmaids

And you thought deciding on the guest list was tricky. Lord Alfred Tennyson had the gift of discernment when he said, "A happy bridesmaid makes a happy bride." Be careful about which bridesmaids you pick. Someone will probably be offended — either because you didn't ask her to be a bridesmaid or because you did. After all, this is probably the fifteenth wedding they've been in this year. And they're now at the point where they have to take out a loan just to afford the bridal shower gift, the wedding gift, and the matching dress and shoes in canary yellow that they'll "*definitely* be able to wear again."

I really wanted to have my best friends from college stand up with me: Dwana, Laura, Kendra, Heidi, and Kim. But I also wanted Scott's daughter, Amy, to be my maid of honor, and my best friend, Amy, to be my matron of honor. Plus I really wanted my Aunt Susy and another friend, Cindy, to participate. That's nine bridesmaids. No way. Maybe if I had a year and a half to plan, but I had barely three months. Try getting nine women — all from different parts of the country — to agree on a dress in that amount of time. The problem was I felt I needed to ask all five of my college friends; otherwise I was afraid I might hurt them by leaving some out. Plus, how could I "rank" them when they are all equally special to me? Knowing them, they probably wouldn't have cared, but I cared. After much painful deliberation, I finally decided against asking any of them. Instead I asked the two Amys, my aunt, and Cindy, who was a friend to both Scott and me.

While it turned out fine, if I could do it again, I would have just had nine bridesmaids. Who cares what anybody would say or think? Of course I realize they would *really* never have been able to find a dress that would work on all of them. But, hey, that's what adds excitement to life.

The point is, stay true to what you want. If you want a dozen bridesmaids, go for it. If you want one, that's fine too. Ask yourself, *Will I regret this choice five years from now?* If the answer is yes, then do whatever you need to do to spare yourself those regrets.

Other Wedding Party Members

A note on children: While children are adorable, they are often unpredictable. Who are we kidding? They're always unpredictable. Those little characters can do the darndest things at the most sacred moments. The most loud, obvious, dramatic child can all of a sudden fall shy, scared, and unwilling to do anything you try to coax out of him or her. They fidget, wave, or shout to Mom, pick their nose, hit the other children in the wedding party, and announce in the middle of communion that they have to go to the bathroom *now*. But other than that, children are truly precious.

Know that if you choose to have children in your wedding party, they may just end up stealing your show. My friend Amy got out of that dilemma by having all her nieces and nephews sing a song together at the beginning of the ceremony.

You may have visions of your flower girl walking serenely down the aisle dropping rose petals a few at a time evenly all the way to the altar. You may end up getting a high-energy girl who flings all the petals at the first two pews she passes. Not so cute; not so romantic, but true to the nature of a child. Just keep in mind that kids will be kids.

Once you've decided to throw caution to the wind and allow children to be members of the wedding party, you will need to deal with the parents of those children. That's when, if you're not careful, your wedding will take a backseat to the child star. Make sure you communicate clearly upfront what you expect—both from the child and the parents.

—Quick Tips—

Don't ask for too many opinions—they'll only confuse you.

Susan, married nine months

One thing you definitely want is to find a handful of people, besides your fiancé, who "get it" and who get you. When you lose yourself in all the planning, those people will be honest with you. They will keep you grounded.

Jeane, married four years

Be careful of asking your sibling's girlfriends to be in your wedding. I asked my brother's girlfriend to be a bridesmaid, then he broke up with her before the wedding! At first I wanted to ask him, "Why couldn't you have waited until after the wedding to break up with her?" Then I realized if he had waited so she could be in the wedding, she would have been immortalized in our photos and videos—something neither my brother nor I would have wanted.

Leslie, married four years

61

FIVE

Harnessing Your Inner Bride

I have a good friend, Laura, who was great to be around during my engagement period. I felt so comfortable speaking with her about my wedding plans.

One day, she really proved her friendship when, as we were walking the track at our health club, she laughed and said, "Okay, earth calling Ginger! Come back to everyday life."

Let's face it, our friends and family can take only so much wedding talk. There are other events going on in the world. Your friends liked you before you became engaged. Your goal is to keep it that way! That means as a bride you need to be sensitive to how much you discuss your plans and with whom you share them. One woman, Kate, discussed a "cringe worthy" moment during her best friend's engagement: "I was astonished at my best friend's transformation. She used to be levelheaded, then our conversations began to revolve around her impending marriage. At one point, we discussed some trivial thing that wasn't coming together—invitations or something. It seemed to me there was an easier approach than the one over which she was stressing. 'Well, do you have to do it that way?' I asked. 'What if you did it this other way?' I'll never forget the comment that followed and the disgusted look she shot at me. 'Kate,' she hissed, 'that's not *etiquette*.' When a down-to-earth girl who previously couldn't have cared less whether or not her clothes matched starts getting defensive about 'etiquette,' you know the world is on its head."

What is it about weddings that cause otherwise lovely, logical women to turn into irrational taskmasters over hairpins, altar decorations, bridesmaid shoes, and the wording of shower invitations? I'll tell you what it is: It's the inner "diva" bride announcing her presence. She shows up with her expectations of perfection and won't leave until we reach them or have caused a feud with everyone within a ten-mile radius.

My father is a minister, and he has told me about brides who have thrown tantrums because their hair wasn't exactly right or because their fiancé joked throughout the rehearsal or because the guest book wasn't placed on the correct table. He was very kind when he told me after I became engaged, "Don't do that."

Choosing Your Battles

Planning my wedding was my opportunity to show the world I was classy and I was throwing an elegant, chic shindig. You can imagine my horror when I discovered Scott didn't understand the meaning of tasteful invitations. We ordered them with no problems. But then I made the mistake of asking him to participate in addressing them. I gave him the inner envelopes. All he had to do was write the first and last names of the guests. When I looked to see how he was progressing, I felt my chest tighten as I watched him write "hi!" and draw a smiley face under the guests' names.

"What are you doing?" I demanded.

"What?"

"Don't 'what' me. Why are you drawing a smiley face?"

"Because I wanted to."

"How many other smiley faces have you drawn?"

"Why?"

My jaw clenched.

"This is an elegant occasion. These are formal invitations. *Formal.* You are not signing someone's stinking yearbook."

"But they know me. I've got to tell them hi."

This was an important lesson for me on choosing your battles. I took a deep breath and told myself, *Let it go, Ginger. It's not the end of the world. This is a time when Scott is excited about wanting to help me. And even though he is not doing it correctly—like he should be—at least he's involved.*

And I did let it go. When picking your battles, here is a good guideline to consider: Does this make an eternal or a temporal difference? So those few guests received smiley faces. They probably chuckled and forgot it. That's temporal. If I would have bashed Scott's character because of what he did, that would have hurt him and our relationship—and that's eternal. Consider anything that builds or burns relationships as eternal. Pretty much anything else is temporal.

The "Weighting" Game

One of my first thoughts after I said "yes" was, *Oh no! I have to get serious about losing weight.* Never mind it was the same twenty pounds I'd been trying to lose since high school. For me it wasn't just about looking slim and svelte in my wedding gown, it was about the fact that Scott was going to see me buck naked on our wedding night—big thighs and all. Argh.

No matter what your size, you probably would like to lose some pounds. I knew if I lost weight I'd feel better about myself. I contacted my physician—who agreed with my assessment!— then I joined Weight Watchers and was successfully able to lose more than twenty pounds (of course I regained it after I got married, but that's a topic for another book). The one good thing was that I didn't do a crash course. I went with an established weight-loss program that also offered accountability. It took me about ten months to lose the weight, but I felt wonderful. Until, of course, I went to try on bridal gowns. Here's a secret that nobody will tell you, that nobody told me. The gown designers label wedding gowns with incorrect sizing tags. If you wear a size 8 dress regularly, you won't take a size 8 wedding dress. You'll need a size 10 or 12. And a size 8 dress will fit on a twig. Isn't that a kicker? Here we brides are, already feeling self-conscious about our size, wanting to slice off serious poundage from our hips and backsides, and these "thoughtful" designers do this to us. Sigh.

Weight Exercise

In his book *A Celebration of Sex for Newlyweds*, noted Christian sex therapist Dr. Douglas Rosenau offers this exercise to try: "Stand nude in front of a full-length mirror. Now observe yourself and resist making any judgments. After observing a few minutes, start with your hair and proceed down to your feet, accepting and describing every one of your body parts with no negative judgments."[1]

I'm not going to lie. This exercise is a tough one—especially if you've battled weight problems at some point in your life, which most women have. The best advice I can give is to decide to be happy with who you are. You will experience enough stress without trying to remake yourself.

I was depressed for days after I went to the first bridal boutique, and I swore I wasn't going to eat again. Of course, that lasted right up until the time I went to McDonald's and ordered just about everything on the left side of the menu—plus a Diet Coke. You need *some* restraint, after all.

If you decide you need to lose some weight, here are some tips I'd like to offer:

- Talk to your physician first. She'll give you some great insight on how much you should lose and how to do that safely.

- Find a group to hold you accountable. There's nothing like stepping on a scale and hearing, "Good girl!" or "Uh oh, what happened this week?" to keep you focused.

- Eat plenty of fruits and vegetables and drink plenty of water (this will also help your complexion).

- Finally, follow my personal guidelines for calorie counting: If it's a neutral color—say milk chocolate—it has no calories.

—Quick Tips—

Try to keep your sense of humor. My uncle, who was my organist, broke a lot of tension when during the rehearsal he played "I'd Rather Have Jesus" as I walked down the aisle.

Eileen, married two years

Stick to your guns. Decide what's really important to you. Let the rest go.

Amy, married five years

—Quick Quip—

I am your God . . . I see all your actions. And I love you because you are beautiful, made in my own image. . . . Do not judge yourself. Do not condemn yourself. Do not reject yourself. . . . Come, come, let me wipe your tears, and let my mouth say . . . I love you, I love you, I love you.[2]

Henri Nouwen

Six

Details, Details

I often thought I would have enjoyed my engagement more if I didn't have to deal with those pesky wedding details — and the resplendent ineptitude of so many customer service people in the wedding industry. To quote a recent bride, "My joy is being robbed in the details!"

If I could impress upon you only one piece of advice in this chapter, it would be this: Trust your gut. If you don't feel completely comfortable with a vendor, don't hire him or her. This is imperative because there is a strong possibility you will regret your decision if you go full steam ahead. Someone who is nice doesn't equal someone who is competent. God gave us that little feeling in the pit of our stomachs for a reason. Call it instinct or intuition, it never lies.

Your Rite of Passage: The Wedding Gown

The thought of choosing a wedding gown causes some brides to break out in hives. This task is not just about finding the right gown; this is about your rite of passage. And as such, you can't pick it out alone. This is a great opportunity to include other special people in the experience. This is also a great first step toward healing estranged relationships. You may read this and think, *Whoa! It's stressful enough wading through aisle after aisle and rack after rack of plastic-covered dresses. Why would I want to add to the stress?* Here's why.

After her engagement, Amy and her mother decided to look for wedding gowns and on a whim, Amy invited her future mother-in-law to join them. That turned out to open the door for a great relationship between Amy and her mother-in-law. "She couldn't believe that I had thought enough of her to include her in that experience," says Amy. Four years later, her mother-in-law still brings up that experience in conversation.

While you will want these women's opinions, the thing to remember is that this is your dress. You want to feel comfortable and special in it. If your mother has her heart set on you wearing her wedding dress and you don't want to, don't. You can thank her for her kind offer, but express to her that you had envisioned a different look for your wedding day. It's okay to have different tastes. It's okay to say no if your Aunt Margaret wants to sew your dress and everyone agrees. You don't have to apologize for your wishes or tastes in clothes. And you don't have to apologize for saying, "No, thank you."

Anna was another bride who asked her mother to join her on the gown search. It started out fine until her mother picked out a traditional, formal gown—everything Anna didn't want. "I'd originally seen it on the rack and I didn't like it," says Anna, "so when Mom brought the dress for me to try on, I didn't say anything. I tried it on." That was a pivotal moment in their relationship, according to Anna, when she stepped out of the dressing room and her mom took in a breath and got teary-eyed. "She loved the dress—and I hated it. I could have caved in because I wanted to please her. But I knew if I wasn't honest with my mom, I'd end up wearing a dress that wasn't my taste or style." Anna finally found the nerve to say, "I'm sorry, Mom, I can't wear this. It just doesn't work for me." It was a tense moment because Anna could see her mother was upset. Yet Anna stood her ground, and her mother accepted her decision. "I think more than anything," says Anna, "it meant a lot that at least we were there together."

Possibly Your Last Rites: Bridesmaids' Dresses

If you expect picking out bridesmaids' dresses to be a win-win situation, you're in for a big surprise. Trying to accommodate everyone's body type in one dress style can call for a referee or professional negotiator at times.

There's nothing that can bring out the inner bridesmaid faster than putting her in a dress she doesn't like.

Amanda knows about this from personal experience. She had seven attendants—all with distinct tastes and definite opinions. "My bridesmaids were not shy about telling me their opinions," says Amanda. "One bridesmaid had big hips, another was heavy chested. My sister didn't want a dress that showed her arms. I didn't necessarily want sleeves on my bridesmaids' dresses, but I ended up going with short, little sleeves because my sister didn't want her *big* arms showing—and she doesn't even have big arms."

You may also harbor grandiose dreams that you can choose a bridesmaid's dress that she'll be able to wear again. This is the reality: Your bridesmaids are *never* going to wear the dresses again. So just buy them knowing that.

Or you can compromise and allow each bridesmaid to pick her own dress. Leslie was a bride who decided to go that route—initially. She told her bridesmaids they could choose whichever dress they wanted to wear as long as it matched her chosen colors. No big deal, she thought. Until she discovered not everyone necessarily has the same clothing tastes she does.

Leslie hated the dress one of her bridesmaids chose. "It was so ugly, I couldn't believe it," Leslie says. "But I couldn't say anything because I had told them they could choose. What was I supposed to say? 'Sorry, everyone *except* you can pick your dress'?" That's when she realized those dresses—as gawky, gaudy, and chiffony as they may be—really do matter. "People would see them. And our photographer would capture them on film. Did I really want to be reminded of her awful dress every time I looked at our wedding album?" Leslie says. As tactfully as possible, she explained to her bridesmaids that she had changed her mind and she really did want them to wear the same dress style—one that she would choose. She apologized for the inconvenience, and everything turned out okay.

A Picture Is Worth a Thousand Bucks

Finding a good photographer is a gift. Choose to skimp on anything else in your wedding *except* your photography. That day will fly by and your memories will be surreal and fuzzy, and the only thing you'll have left to remember in the years to come will be a blender you've never used and your photographs. It's worth spending the extra money to find someone good. That doesn't mean you need to find the most expensive photographer. But this is usually a case in which you get what you pay for. If your sister's neighbor's cousin "dabbles" in photography, stay away.

And if you visit a photographer, you can ask all those questions the etiquette books give you, but in the end, take a good, hard, critical look at his work and listen to what your instincts tell you.

My instincts told me to run away *fast*. But because we had less than three months to plan a wedding two states away in a small town, I was stuck. I should have listened to that nagging feeling because it proved itself right.

I cried when I saw our photographs—and I had no one else to blame. I said yes when I should have said no. My one consolation was that I've talked to a number of brides who felt the same way. They didn't listen to that inner voice either.

Fortunately, Scott and I had plenty of friends and family who also took photos. Here are a few other photographic ideas we ran across:

Ask a friend who is an amateur photographer to take photos of events your "hired" photographer won't be attending: the rehearsal and rehearsal dinner; bridesmaid luncheon; any prewedding outings with your bridal party (i.e. group manicures); prewedding preparations such as at the hair salon and getting dressed the day of the wedding; and the final hours of the reception. Ask someone to do a photo journal. Tell your friend upfront you'll pay for all photo developing. Then get her a nice thank-you gift for her time.

Put out disposable cameras on each table at your reception. While this isn't a new idea, the important point is to make sure each camera has a ready flash. Scott and I purchased cameras that had flashes the "photographer" had to prep. Most guests aren't going to "get it." At least, ours didn't—which meant when we developed the film, half the photos didn't come out. Make sure to get the point-and-shoot kind.

Ask a friend who knows most of the wedding party, your family, and the guests to assist the photographer by checking off the list of photos you want. Also, your friend can point out special photo opportunities for candids of special guests.

Once you receive your photos from your "professional" photographer, put the proofs on a website so out-of-town folks can see them and order any they want. I know two brides who did this, and it worked out well. Christine got married in New England—too far for me to attend—and since I don't see her often, I knew I wouldn't get to see her wedding photos either. But because she put them on the Internet, I was able to enjoy her wedding. She numbered each photo, too, so if I wanted to order any, I could e-mail her the numbers.

Consider listening to music while you have your posed photos taken. Jeane's fiancé, Tyson, gathered a CD compilation of romantic music to have playing while the photographer was shooting. "It made a huge difference," Jeane says. "The atmosphere was fun. And taking the pictures became more relaxing and enjoyable."

How to Get What You Don't Need: Your Gift Registry

This is your chance to ask for everything you've ever wanted but will probably never use: china sets and cappuccino or pasta makers, for instance. Dream big, and don't worry about offending anyone with your registry choices. Half your guests won't use the list you so carefully chose and almost broke the engagement over anyway. Instead, many guests will forego the registry to give you a present they've determined is much more "you," such as a ceramic swan candy dish.

My problem with registering was that it added to my already overwhelming stress. When Scott and I went to the store to register, our registry consultant handed me a packet the size of a phone book to wade through. It had page after page of what we *should* register for. *But I don't want a crystal gravy boat,* I kept saying to myself. I was forced to choose a china pattern for dishes I would use once every decade but would still be thrilled over for my lifetime. I was having enough difficulty choosing my wedding colors!

There are a few good things about registering, however:

1. This is a great opportunity to get your fiancé involved in the wedding. Scott and I chose two national stores that both offered price scanner guns — Scott's dream toy. He was happy; I was happy. We were doing something together. Of course, he kept adding items to the register, then deleting them — just because he could. (Maybe that's why we received four mini food processors.)

2. Try also to register in a store that has a hardware section for your fiancé. Let's face it, your man is probably more excited about tools than towels, and he can register to his little heart's content.

3. If you can survive registering with your fiancé without throttling him or breaking your engagement, your marriage has a great chance of surviving and thriving. "We had one of our most heated arguments while we were registering," says Janie. "The only good thing about it was that another couple was in the same department arguing."

4. You may discover interesting tidbits about your fiancé you never knew. When Scott lifted a beautiful crystal candy dish and wanted to include that on the list, I balked. "Why do you want to register for crystal? You aren't even interested in crystal," I told him. "I know," he said. "But my grandma had a candy dish similar to this, and I always got candy out of it when I was growing up. I'd like it for the memories." That candy dish is now sitting in our house.

The Hoopla after the Ceremony: Your Reception

Nowadays, it seems everyone expects receptions to include full-serve meals. If you don't want to do that or if you don't have the budget for it, don't panic. Many receptions have cake, nuts, and punch. And that's okay. Anna and her fiancé, John, chose to have a sundae buffet at a local park. It was in the afternoon, it was informal. It was them. You don't have to let someone else dictate how you should have your reception, where you should have it, or what should or should not be served. "My mother was upset because she said everyone will expect to be fed," Anna says. "But why do people go to weddings anyway? For the food? No. If that's why they were attending, then I didn't want them there."

Regardless of what other people expect, this party is yours, and if you are paying the cost, you have the right to go with your desires.

If someone else is paying for the reception, however, you may need to compromise. My friend Trina wanted to have an informal, by invitation only cookout at her parents' house. Everyone seemed to be fine with that except her mother. "You cannot invite hundreds of guests and then not invite them all to the reception," she said. But Trina was on a strict budget, so when Trina's mother offered to pay for an afternoon reception with cake and punch for everyone, then hold the informal cookout later in the evening, Trina agreed.

My friend Victorya also had to come up with a compromise when some of her family adamantly opposed having alcohol at the reception. The problem was she had invited some guests who expected alcohol. She wanted to please everyone and still have an enjoyable reception, so after discussing it at length, Victorya and her fiancé decided to have a cash bar. They would provide champagne for a toast, then if a wedding guest wanted another drink, it was available at the guest's cost.

Here's the bottom line: This is *your* wedding. If you want to have dancing and a taco buffet and circus clowns—and even if you don't want to—let it be a decision you can be okay about.

100 Ways to Ooh and Aah: Bridal Showers

True confession: I hated my bridal showers. I mean, overall, they were lovely. But I think I would have liked them more if

I didn't have to sit up front and open presents while everyone looked on and oohed and aahed. Plus everyone is watching your reaction. "Oh! A . . . um . . . cow-shaped cookie jar. Oh, and it moos when you open it. How clever. This is *just* what I wanted! I love it. Thank you." I mean, how many different ways can you express "genuine" delight over a household gift? Give me chocolate, and I'm rapturous; give me a salad spinner, and I'm not so much . . .

Yet this is part of being a gracious bride. If you really think about what these women do when purchasing a gift, wrapping it, and presenting it to you, it can be overwhelming—both for them in their preparations and for you as you recognize their thoughtfulness. They are wanting to share in your new life by giving you something to help prepare you for the road ahead. How a blender does that, I'm still not sure, but it's true.

When my Aunt Ruby, however, presented me with a quilt she had made by hand, I was truly touched. "You didn't have to do this," I told her.

"But I wanted to," she replied.

That's when I realized what a true gift I had received—not just from Aunt Ruby, but from all those women. I had been "showered" by the goodness of people. What a self-esteem builder. They cared enough about me to go out of their way to be part of my life. Those women were there to celebrate my journey into a new life. That was an amazing revelation.

The Compare Snare

At some point you may find yourself comparing what you do to what other brides have done. For instance, while Susan was planning her wedding, she and her fiancé, David, attended the wedding of a bride whose groom was the son of a florist. She had more than a thousand roses in the chapel. The wedding was elegant—and it was in the same place as Susan was having hers. "I thought, *Oh no, are we doing enough? Is ours too simple?*

Have we scaled back too much?" Susan says. "I had to catch myself from trying to emulate someone else's wedding."

Take heart, your wedding will never be as grandiose as some, and it will never be as gaudy as others. As long as you make your wedding *yours* and don't worry over what others have done, your day will be wonderful. And that's what counts.

— Quick Tips —

The library is a great place to find bridal books.

Eileen, married two years

Consider taking a pair of tennis shoes and dressing them up with lace to wear to your reception. Otherwise your feet will kill you!

Jeane, married four years

Your bridesmaids' dresses don't have to match.

Lisa, married three years

In the invitations to all out-of-town guests, include any pertinent phone numbers as well as a map of how to get to the town, church, reception hall, and hotel.

Eileen, married two years

Read the fine print on those contracts! Ask about any additional charges such as delivery, taxes, tips, setup and cleanup, and rental charges. Does the band, photographer, deejay expect you to provide a meal? Better to know up front than to be surprised!

Madelyn, married two years

Make sure your videographer knows which
button to hit to record. If you don't have a
professional videographer capture your wedding,
you may end up with a blank tape! My husband's
uncle filmed ours. We got a nice opener of the
church, then it went blank. He didn't realize
which button to push.

Lisa, married three years

Consider silk flowers or flowers that dry well for
your bouquet so you can keep it.

Jeane, married four years

Before your wedding day, make sure you ask
people to man the gift table, cut the cake, and pass
out the rice/birdseed/bubbles.

Eileen, married two years

You're going to have your dress, you're going to
have your cake, your fiancé is going to have his
tux. Everything else you can get at Wal-Mart, so
don't worry about it.

Jeane, married four years

No, you do not have to have an organist play
during the ceremony. If you want your brother
to play a kazoo while you walk down the aisle,
doggone it, that's your prerogative.

Jennifer, married four years

Don't be afraid to send things back. Remember,
you're paying for the service or the invitation, so
you need to be satisfied.

Amy, married four years

— Quick Quips —

At one of my bridal showers, keeping with tradition, a woman kept all my ribbons to glue to a paper plate for me to use as a faux bouquet at my rehearsal. The only problem was she glued each ribbon to a separate plate. I ended up with more than a dozen single-ribboned plate bouquets.

Kay, married three years

If you and your fiancé have trouble agreeing on wedding details, you may want to consider bringing in a third party. Scott wanted the theme from *Love Story* played during our wedding. While it is no doubt a beautiful piece of music, it came from a movie in which the woman dies at the end. Not exactly an image I wanted in my mind — or the minds of our guests! — while I was walking down the aisle. Not that I'm superstitious, but why chance it? I kept trying to explain this to Scott, but he just wasn't getting it until I spoke with his brother, who told him, "Man, you want a death song played at your wedding?" That got through.

Ginger, married three years

SEVEN

Countdown
to the Big Day

It was a beautiful Sunday afternoon, and Scott and I were headed to the Around the Clock diner for some brunch. It had been a long week of planning, working overtime, and dealing with some family "disturbances." I was exhausted. At the restaurant the hostess seated us in a booth right in the middle of the main thoroughfare. Everything was fine, pleasant actually. Until I opened the menu. Then my eyes glazed over as I saw several pages of egg options. We're not even talking about waffles, oatmeal, pancakes, and other breakfast extravaganza.

And something snapped. *Does* everything *have to be a major decision?* I thought. Then I burst into tears.

"Excuse me," I said as I grabbed a napkin, covered my face, and headed for the ladies' room. Of course, on the way I walked past the salad bar—or should I say, slid past. I had stepped on some ranch dressing that had spilled.

That was only the beginning. Hoping for some privacy in the restroom, I entered a stall and pulled as much toilet paper from the roll as my hand could hold. I didn't even remove it from the roll, since I figured I would use a lot. Sobbing and blowing my nose was okay—until I heard two teenagers enter the restroom. Teenagers don't just use the facility and leave. They gab . . . and giggle . . . and grate on nerves! I knew I couldn't stay in the ladies' room much longer, so I took a deep breath, clutched the rest of the toilet paper, and walked out the door. Blessedly, I bypassed the ranch dressing still on the floor.

I made it back to the table and thought I was collected enough to order—anything but eggs—when Scott was suddenly overtaken by a bout of compassion. He laid his hand on my arm and said, "Was it something I did?"

That was all it took. The floodgates opened, and I began to cry again. I couldn't even say no; I could only shake my head and watch him register relief.

The waitress came, and left, quickly. The patrons glanced at our table and whispered as I wept into my menu.

Every woman who has cried knows that if you start to cry you will be unable to stop. So I pretty much cried through the entire meal.

I wish I could say that was the only time I broke down at the overwhelming sense of stress, panic, doubt, expectations, and financial worries. But alas, I gave in to tears several more times—one on the way to a premarital counseling session, and one after we left a bakery with our doughnuts in hand.

It's My Wedding, and I'll Cry If I Want To!

There is a strong possibility that at some point you will find yourself in a similar place in which you'll need to cry. That's okay. You have now entered the Breakdown Zone—that secret zone nobody talks about for fear you'll elope and cause them to miss the free dinner and dancing at your reception. Everyone enters this zone for a time to cry, then they feel better. Give yourself permission to cry. Let the tears fall. Sob if you want.

One bride, Lisa, always saw crying as a weakness. Yet when she was alone, she found herself thinking about how different her family unit would be after the wedding, and that made her cry. "It really surprised me because I don't cry!" she says.

You can push them down, you can tell yourself, *Crying does no good, snap out of it*. But eventually those tears will make their appearance — and they will choose the most inopportune, embarrassing, awkward place and time to visit. For me, it was at the overly crowded Around the Clock diner during Sunday brunch. For another bride, it happened to be during the rehearsal dinner.

Your tears won't change any of the prewedding stress, panic, worry, or situations, but they will help you cope better and relieve some of the tension. And you don't have to explain them to anyone.

Arguments

Scott and I had just come from meeting with the deejay, and we were both in a mood. It started before we even went to meet her. I was upset because she had asked us to have our list of "must have" songs ready to present to her so she could make sure she had them — the ones that include the couple's first dance, the father-daughter dance, and the like. Well, we didn't have it — not because I was ill-prepared, but because my sweet beloved would not help me make the list. I kept telling him we needed to have it ready, but he wouldn't listen, saying, "She doesn't need it right now. Let me think about it."

So we sat in the deejay's office with nothing prepared. And both of us were ticked off. I'm sure that was a most unpleasant meeting for that deejay. Every question she asked was met with silence from me and barely a grunt from Scott. It was miserable, and we both received an earful once we left.

Author C. J. Ducasse said, "To speak of 'mere words' is much like speaking of 'mere dynamite.'" He's right. When we get into arguments, many times we regret the things we fling. On the bright side, I wasn't the first gal to argue with her fiancé. Karen and Kevin got into an argument so heated they did not speak to each other for several days — all over the type of invitations they would send to the guests. Lisa and Bryan had a doozy of a "discussion" over handy wipes.

The best thing these women and I have discovered is to be honest about how you feel yet to weigh carefully your words. Author Pearl Hurd said, "Handle words carefully, for they have more power than atomic bombs." And words, like bombs, can't be taken back. If you're too emotional, wait to discuss the issue. And if you're tired, wait until you've both rested since fatigue only escalates an argument.

You may try to avoid having arguments, but stressful situations tend to push the envelope. As one married man, Erik, states: "You can't escape it; engagements and weddings require inordinate amounts of patience. It's about two lives coming together into one. Look out! Boom, bang, crash."

This is a great time to learn how much your fiancé is willing to compromise, how much you are willing to compromise, how much he is willing to let you compromise, and vice versa. Those arguments can help you decipher what's really important and whether or not your priorities are in the right place.

They can also reveal deeper issues. Angel discovered this when she and her fiancé, Jim, got into an argument about whether or not to serve sandwiches at their reception. "I'd done all this research on the best deal for our budget, and Jim wanted us to talk to his sister," Angel says. "While I like his sister, I felt hurt. I felt as if he didn't trust my judgment, as if he didn't trust me. But that argument took us into deeper ground, because we dealt with my trust issues and got some things cleared up on that front. It ended up being a blessing."

Guilt and the Disease to Please

Planning for a wedding is time-consuming and can feel all-encompassing, even to the point where some friends won't understand why you've suddenly become invisible from their presence. You may begin to feel guilty because you've been focusing exclusively on the wedding. Between panicking over the budget, the bridesmaid dresses, weight loss, and trimming down the guest list, you can include guilt in the plethora of emotions you will probably experience. You may feel guilt over not hiring your mom's best friend to bake the cake. Or over not asking your sister to sing in the wedding. *The Don't Sweat Guide for Weddings* talks about the real meaning of guilt: "Sometimes, guilt can act as a good force, since it keeps us in check regarding the feelings of others. Most of the time, however, our emotions of guilt are actually fears of rejection. We are afraid that if we let someone down, that if we don't make them happy, we will lose their approval."[1]

Shannon, who had four months to plan her wedding, felt guilty because she wasn't spending time with her friends. "Sure they made some comments," says Shannon. "But I realized I couldn't please everybody. Planning a wedding is a huge task and I had to draw a boundary—or I wouldn't get things completed!"

At some point you will probably hear about someone who does not agree with a decision you have made. My organist hated the songs I chose for the preceremony. That's okay. I had to remember that it didn't matter; the wedding was mine, not hers. But you hold the ace card—you are the bride and the final decision is yours.

You don't have to defend, explain, apologize, or feel guilty.

The reality is that no matter how hard you try to make things perfect and to please everyone, someone somewhere will refuse to cooperate. I'm sure someone hated the bridesmaids' dresses

I chose or someone thought, *I'd never do it that way.* That's fine. Let them think that—they will anyway, and there is nothing you can do to stop them. Madelyn's grandfather wasn't happy that he was asked to read a Scripture passage out of a different translation than he preferred. Your mother-in-law may get upset because you've chosen not to serve chicken at your reception meal. Why wear yourself out by wasting your energy on other people's fastidious opinions? You'll only end up being exhausted, irritated, and joy-depleted. Several times when I became anxious about what others were thinking, I had to give myself a pep talk: *Buck up, Ginger. Stand true. They'll get over it.* It worked.

Manipulation

It started out as a beautiful morning. Amelia had planned to have a small reception at her parents' house after her wedding. To prepare for the reception, Amelia's mother had hired a landscaping service to mow the lawn, fix the flowers, and make everything perfect for that afternoon. They showed up in the morning and started to work.

Unbeknownst to Amelia or her mother, Amelia's grandmother stepped outside to "supervise" the landscapers. That's when she told them to "dig up all these old flowers" from the front yard, which they did. So the lawn was mowed, and where the flowers once bloomed, there was now only dirt.

After everyone discovered what Amelia's grandmother had done and expressed their distress, Amelia's grandmother said, "Well, if I'm such a bad person, I guess I just won't come to the wedding."

Know anyone like that? If not, you're a rarity. Trust me, you'll more than likely encounter at least one person who'll pull the martyrdom act with you. That someone will probably try to strong-arm you into doing what he or she wants. And when you say no, they may "threaten" you with not attending your wedding. Call their bluff. That means you kindly but graciously say, "I'm really sorry you feel that way. However, if that's what you think is best, then I understand." They'll snap out of it and straighten up. And if not, you don't want them at your special event anyway.

That's what happened to Madelyn. Her mother-in-law, a strict, conservative Christian, discovered there would be dancing at the wedding—something she opposed. When "dancing" was brought up casually as Madelyn and her fiancé were discussing their wedding plans, Madelyn's mother-in-law said, "Dancing is a sin. How can you call yourselves Christians and dance?" The mother-in-law fought hard for her case; she used tears and angry words—then she brought out the big guns: "If you choose to have dancing at your reception, then I won't attend." There was a moment of stunned silence, then Madelyn's fiancé said, "Mom, if that's what you choose to do, so be it. But we're having dancing at our wedding." Madelyn's mother-in-law attended the wedding.

The Art of Compromise

On the other hand, there will be times when you'll want to consider the wishes of a family member or friend. This is especially true when your family or your fiancé's family includes a divorced or feuding couple. There's a time to stand firm, yet there's also a time to honor another person's desires. You can be creative, just be discerning as well about your considerations. After all, if a pushy sister gets her way with one thing, she may expect to get her way on everything.

Something else to consider is the root of their desire. Does your maid of honor want you to hold an afternoon wedding because she hates getting up early? On the other hand, did she suggest it because she knew her work schedule wouldn't allow her the flexibility to take a day off to travel to Hawaii for your wedding?

Jan and her fiancé, Adam, decided to compromise with her mother, who had pushed for an extended guest list and serving food at the reception — two things Jan didn't want. So she extended a compromise: food or people. "I told her," says Jan, "you can invite the people you want and we will have the reception we want, or you get the reception with the meal, but you don't get to invite your full guest list." Jan felt strongly about those options. She was able to say no, yet compromise in some area and still retain her dignity. Her mother chose the people. It caused some tension and fuss, but in the end many of those people her mother invited never attended the wedding.

Another area of compromise may come with your fiancé. Amy was surprised when she discovered she would have to compromise with her fiancé, Trei, over their formal silverware pattern. "He was shocked that I didn't even consider registering for formal sterling silver!" Amy admits. Since it was so important to him, she decided to register for it. They went through a catalog of a hundred different formal silverware patterns. "We said pick your favorite and your least favorite fork pattern," says Amy. "Out of the hundred different forks, our choices were the exact opposite! We just looked at each other like, *You're kidding, right?*" So they compromised. Amy chose the everyday silverware and Trei picked the formalware. "I let him pick the crystal too, since the fancy items really mattered to him. That was really surprising, but it taught me an important lesson in compromising because you love someone."

Obviously the wedding day is the fulfillment of your dreams. You don't have to feel as though you must deviate from that. If you feel strongly about something, just say no. However, some things truly won't make a difference several years down the road, even though they may seem as if they're earth-shattering decisions in that moment. You may discover it's possible to honor your loved ones' wishes *and* your own. My mother is shy when it comes to being in front of people. The thought of getting up in front of everyone and dancing with my father terrified her. As much as I wanted her to dance with my dad, I realized that it would cause her undue stress. I let it go. I was disappointed, but I knew I needed to honor my mom's desire. Did that destroy the reception? No. In fact, I don't recall anyone saying anything about it. We all survived.

The Art of Saying No

You may be surprised to discover that people have strong opinions regarding how you should handle your wedding. Regardless of what others think, feel, say, threaten, or do, you and your husband-to-be are the ones who count the most.

Eighteen-year-old Sandi wanted to be married outdoors in front of a small gathering. Instead, she ended up having a church wedding in front of three hundred guests. During her engagement, a friend found cloth napkins for the reception, so she bought three hundred of them and presented them to Sandi as a gift. Nice gesture — except the napkins needed to be ironed, folded, and transported to the reception site, something Sandi's friend didn't offer to do. So Sandi, her fiancé, and their mothers spent hours working on the cloth napkins. "I didn't even want the napkins!" says Sandi. "And I was fuming the whole time I was ironing and folding. I should have said no."

Saying no is especially important with regard to vendors. They can be persuasive. Stick to your guns! Even if it's the "deal of a lifetime." What they suggest may be nice and elegant and wonderful. But if it's not in your budget or not your style, then just say, "No, thank you." Trust me, they won't take it personally. You — and your choices — deserve to be respected. So stand firm.

Doubts and Grieving Your Singleness

You may be so focused on planning your wedding and looking forward to the wonderful days of marriage that what you're leaving behind won't be a glimmer in your mind. Yet there may be moments when you wonder about what you're giving up: those days of privacy, independence, and freedom. There may be moments when you look at your sweetheart and think, *This is what I'm going to live with for the rest of my life? What am I thinking?* Or you may wonder, *Am I really ready for this?* After all, marriage is a deeper level of commitment and responsibility than you've ever had. It calls for you to put all your eggs in one basket, to go for broke, to give it all you've got, and every other cliché you can come up with. And if you're entering a marriage with a ready-made family because of children, or if you want to start a family, double those clichés.

Husbands and children have a way of squeezing every ounce of independence out of you. And privacy is a thing of the past. Acknowledge that those doubts are a normal part of the grieving process. And take some time to make the most of doing the things you can do alone. You can choose your own ice cream flavor and eat it all yourself. You can spend an entire day at the mall and not tell anyone where you are. You don't have to justify why you spent $300 on clothes. You can eat cereal for supper.

It's okay to take some time to grieve—and revel in!—your singleness. You can thank God for the blessings you have right now during your final days of this life season.

Doubts and What Your Fiancé Is Thinking

I remember several conversations Scott and I had in which he asked, "Are you going to get tired of me? Are you going to leave me?" I had to give him credit: I was wondering that about him too, but he verbalized his thoughts.

Rest assured, at some point your fiancé will also experience doubts. I would worry if he didn't doubt. He may be fearful that he'll fail at marriage. After all, those divorce statistics are enough to scare anyone. This is an opportunity for you to reassure him you'll love him no matter what. Shower him with attention. Go on dates and don't even mention the wedding. Do something he enjoys such as attending a hockey game or practicing golf at the driving range.

Try not to place more value on the wedding than on your fiancé. Your wedding is a big event, a big celebration, but it's not your marriage. If you have a choice between working on the wedding and spending time with him, make the choice to be with him.

Premarital Counseling

With everything else on your to-do list for the wedding, you may feel as if premarital counseling is a waste of time. *After all*, you may figure, *we've dated long enough to know each other*. Or you may think, *Why counseling? We love each other. We get along well. We don't need it*. Yet most of the women I spoke with went through some sort of premarital counseling and felt it was helpful. Typically the counselor will ask you questions to get you thinking.

Scott and I went to premarital counseling. Before our first session, our counselor gave us some questionnaires to fill out and return to him so he could evaluate them before our meeting. When Scott and I met with him, he informed us that we were compatible in most of our areas. Scott and I looked at each other relieved. I think we may have felt subconsciously that the counselor might tell us, "You're not right for each other. Run away—fast!"

He didn't, which was nice of him. But he did give us a caution. "I notice on your evaluations you marked each other as extremely stubborn. So while you agree in that area, you'll want to be aware that you may butt heads on some give-and-take issues." We smiled and nodded, still thinking, *Whew! He didn't tell us we were wrong for each other*.

89

I have to say that particular observation has made a world of difference in my marriage. I'm still stubborn and Scott is still *unreasonably* bullheaded, but it helps me to be aware of it as I try to help him change his mind.

Esther and her fiancé, Dale, appreciated their premarital counseling experiences. "One of the best things we did was to write out our family tree and each member's medical history," she says. "Dale had a right to know if I had some disease or mental illness that ran in my family because I could end up with those things, and he would need to decide before we got married if he was up to the possibility of dealing with that." The genetics are telling: diabetes, cancer, bipolar disorder, ADHD, epilepsy, and the list goes on. This especially helps when you discuss having children, which you need to do before your wedding.

Let me encourage you to schedule premarital counseling. Think of it as an investment in your future—the future that's beyond your wedding day.

— Quick Tips —

On arguments: My rule of thumb is the twenty-four-hour rule. If something's bothering you, you have up to twenty-four hours to bring it up—with grace. If you don't handle it within that time frame, let it go.

Judy, married thirty-three years

Be careful of comparisons. Realize the idea that "the grass is always greener" in some other relationship isn't always as it seems. The grass may be greener on the other side, but you don't know how much work you would have to put into the grass to keep it that way!

Mary, married five years

—Quick Quip—

All adventures, especially into new territory, are scary.

Sally Ride, astronaut

EIGHT

Sex and the Single Girl

Finally, after spending the evening with his family, Scott took me back to my apartment, where I invited him in. What luck! My roommate wasn't home. We'd have the whole place to ourselves. Scott and I hadn't seen each other for a week—and he looked sexy in his tight jeans and green shirt that brought out the green in his eyes.

"You look really nice," Scott said, leaning in to me.

"So do you," I replied.

"*Really* nice," Scott whispered back.

I led him to the couch. Then I lit a few candles and turned on some music. The setting was perfect . . . for trouble.

We were in love, we were in a committed relationship, and we knew we were eventually getting married. And we wanted each other—desperately.

It would be so easy.

Fortunately, my roommate surprised us and came home early from her date.

But there were times after I moved into my own apartment, sans the roommate, when Scott and I were truly alone — with no possibility of someone coming home and surprising us.

The hands do a little exploring; the bodies get a little closer; the kissing moves downward. You get the picture.

What's the Big Deal?

Sex. Whether you're excited, eager, anxious, or nauseated about it, it is at least on your mind. Trust me, it's on your fiancé's mind too.

Now that you know you're getting married to the man you love, those sexual temptations get turned up a notch. Now is the time to recommit to waiting it out — whether you are a virgin or have been sexually active. Yes, it's tough to remain sexually self-controlled. But it's important.

Why? What's the problem with having sex before you're married? Most of our culture views premarital sex as normal, even irresistible. After all, you love each other, you're in a committed relationship, and sex is the way to share your love.

While that sounds good, the reality is that there are consequences to being sexually active with someone who isn't your husband — even if he's going to be your husband. Sex is such a vulnerable, intimate experience that if it's misused — meaning if you participate in the activity outside marriage — it will adversely affect you for the rest of your life. "Sexual freedom" really isn't free — it can carry some heavy costs.

While AIDS is the big scare, we can't forget those hundreds of other sexually transmitted diseases you can get, or even the pesky annoyances — herpes, genital warts. Try explaining that to your husband.

There's a reason God wants us to remain sexually pure and self-controlled before marriage. It's because God created sex to be a soul connection. It's the process by which you become one with another person. You give something away to that other person that you can never get back.

In her book *Inviting God to Your Wedding*, Martha Williamson describes it this way:

> When you get involved with someone—and certainly when you are intimate with someone—it's like gluing two pieces of wood together. Then when you finally pull the wood apart, it doesn't come off clean. Each takes a little piece of the other away with it. The more relationships you have and the more sex you have, the more pieces of other people you are carrying around with you. And unfortunately, by the time you get married, the joy of sex and the thrill of discovery can be significantly diminished.
>
> I am not making a moral judgment here. Sexual activity before marriage quite simply has the effect of bringing a lot of ghosts to the marriage bed. Period. That can result in guilt, jealousy, sexual dysfunction, and even a nagging sense of just not "being present" during lovemaking. I can remember talking to a number of girlfriends who, after they were married, remembered their wedding night with some remorse as "just another night like the ones that came before." Of more concern were women who expected the marriage ceremony itself to somehow magically erase their history.[1]

The reality is that every time you have sex with someone, you're also sleeping with everyone with whom that person has slept. That makes for a rather crowded bed. And that's like playing Russian roulette—that bullet will eventually hit its mark.

Past Sexual History

If you don't have one, you are ahead of the game. Jeane didn't. She came to her husband as a blank slate. "My husband, Tyson, is the best lover I've ever had! He's the only lover I've ever had," says Jeane. "I don't have to worry about flashbacks to other persons. It was amazing to know you are coming to your husband pure, that you haven't been with anybody else."

If you have a sexual history, you need to share that with your fiancé—preferably before you get married. Some people don't feel the need to share this with their significant other because they feel it's none of their business—what's in the past is exactly that and doesn't need to be exposed or rehashed. However, the problem with that becomes a trust issue when your beloved finally does find out—and he will. Then you'll really have a problem on your hands. As your spouse, he has the right to know about your past—and you have the right to know about his. You don't have to bring up the nitty-gritty details. But he does have the right to know whether you're a virgin or not! And how many partners you've had.

The sad part of having a sexual history is that your memory will become fine-tuned. Heather Jamison knows this truth: She and her boyfriend, Brian, became sexually intimate. They married—but those premarital experiences wreaked havoc on their relationship. In her article "Haunted by Premarital Sex" in *Marriage Partnership* magazine, Heather writes,

> We got married to cover the visible consequences—pregnancy— but the emotional and spiritual consequences of our sin became more evident as time progressed. . . . We began to see our premarital relationship for what it really was—counterfeit intimacy. After the layers of deception were peeled away, we discovered a marriage rooted in instant gratification and self-serving pleasures.[2]

Obviously some experiences are going to have a greater impact on your relationship than others. In their book *One Flesh*, Amelia and Greg Clarke write: "It is dangerous to underestimate the importance of even short-lived or seemingly minor sexual encounters. Sex affects us at a deep level, and its impact is felt for many years to come."[3]

So what can you do to help release some of your history's hold over your current and most important relationship? The Clarkes suggest three steps:

1. Decide together how you will talk about your past experiences.
2. Recognize that your first sexual experiences are likely to have had a major impact on how you think and feel about sex. This is especially true if you were not responsible for your past sexual experiences — such as in the case of sexual abuse or date rape. Your mind is a powerful force and can continue to hold you hostage.
3. Pray and recognize that God is willing to forgive sexual sin and wants you to pursue pure living from now on.[4]

Mental Replay

Every time you have a sexual experience outside marriage, you make a mental tape that has this annoying way of replaying itself and interfering with your sex life once you get married. You may experience guilt or regret, which can rob you of the joy of the moment. Not to mention those nasty comparisons. What if your husband doesn't kiss or touch you in the exciting way a former lover did? You'll rob yourself of the joy of knowing your husband intimately. Why set up a competition in the bedroom? Not to mention, sex is a deeply emotional experience. However, the more partners you have, the less emotion you'll feel. In other words, you'll rob yourself of the joy of experiencing a deep emotional bond with your husband.

You can seek forgiveness from your husband and from God, yet the forgetting will be much harder. In his book *Sheet Music,* Dr. Kevin Leman discusses the reality of fighting sexual flashbacks: "The things we want to repress and not think about are usually the things that pop up in our minds during the most inappropriate times."[5] While you can't erase those tapes, you can choose not to allow them access to your current relationship.

Other Reasons for Abstinence

To be fair, I admit I'm probably not the best role model for abstinence. While Scott and I were committed to remaining pure with each other, the reality is there were many times we struggled. It took strength and a lot of determination not to have sex with Scott. It's not easy. I'm not going to tell you I wasn't tempted to "go all the way" before my wedding day. Nor am I going to tell you I was perfectly innocent. There were times when I pushed the envelope. Really pushed the envelope. And there were times when I allowed Scott to push the envelope.

Your husband is worthy of your purity. And while being a virgin is a state I recommend to all brides, I realize not everyone is in that state. Our culture and peer pressure make it difficult. Everywhere you turn, you're bombarded with ideas and sights that say, "Go ahead, if it feels good, do it. What's the big deal?"

Yet there were a few things that kept me from giving something to my fiancé that was reserved strictly for my husband:

1. Scott and I discussed the reality of the physical side of our relationship and what that meant. One of the most romantic things he said to me was, "I'm attracted to you—but more than anything, I want to respect you. And that means we don't have sex before we are married." He wanted to respect my desire to remain pure before my wedding night. So he and I discussed boundaries for what was and was not acceptable for us.

2. While I was engaged to Scott and had every intention of marrying him—after all, we had set a date and had begun to plan and prepare for the wedding—I also knew there was a slim chance we might not get married. I

knew several women who had gotten right up to the week before the wedding, and then the groom took off or they called it off. Does the movie *Runaway Bride* mean anything here? This is one area we brides don't like to consider, but it pays to recognize that something could happen to halt the wedding.

3. I am a romantic at heart. And there was nothing more romantic than to be able to give my body as a present to my husband on our wedding night. I wanted to let Scott know he was so important that I waited to give him something I had shared with no one else.

4. The most important reason for waiting was that Scott and I are both Christ followers. We followed what the Bible says about not engaging in physical union with another person until marriage. First Corinthians 6:18 says, "Run away from sexual sin! No other sin so clearly affects the body as this one does. For sexual immorality is a sin against your own body." Galatians 5:19 (NIV) says, "The acts of the sinful nature are obvious: sexual immorality, impurity . . . I warn you . . . that those who live like this will not inherit the kingdom of God." Obviously God takes sexual purity seriously, so I figured I should too.

Cohabiting

If you are living together, you may want to reconsider this until you get married. I'm sure you're well aware of the divorce statistics in our society. But were you aware that those statistics double for couples who live together before marriage? Numerous studies have been done, and they all come up with the same conclusion: Cohabiting outside marriage is a death knoll for couples who get married. In his book *Buyers, Renters & Freeloaders*, nationally acclaimed clinical psychologist Willard Harley writes, "Marriages following cohabitation are almost inevitably doomed." According to Harley, these couples have a "rental agreement" mind-set. Their relationship is like a lease, which they continue based on a trial basis. "When couples who live together before marriage do decide to marry," he writes, "it's not because they are willing to improve their level of care. They marry because the arrangement worked out so well they are willing to sign a long-term lease. [Yet] they're still operating under the renter's agreement."[6]

The Benefits of Abstinence

Sex is a wonderful part of marriage, yet it's not the only part. The foundation you lay in those other arenas before your marriage will only strengthen your relationship. If you take away the sexual side, you'll discover what you're left with.

Because Scott and I chose not to pursue the physical side of our relationship during our engagement, our time was spent talking and getting to know each other. In other words, we were laying a foundation for friendship, something that would be a stronger tie than sex. We shared an intimacy that came from meaningful, intimate conversations. And we discovered a depth to our conversations and were able to enjoy each other's company without the pressure of it going somewhere.

And the physical side we did engage in—kissing and holding hands—became treasured gifts we gave each other. Now that we are married, we still hold tightly to these aspects of our physical relationship.

We also realized that if we could keep our commitment to abstain during our engagement, then it would be a stronger commitment to abstain from other people once we were married. I realized if Scott respected me enough during our dating days to keep us pure, I could trust him to keep our relationship pure while we were married.

But what if you and your fiancé are already engaged in that aspect of your relationship? As difficult as it may be, have a straight talk with your fiancé and tell him the truth: You and he need to wait until your wedding night. One, it will be exciting to give him something "new." Two, the wedding night will be truly special—not just another night.

Even if he gets upset, stick to your guns. My friend Gina told her fiancé, Jeff, that they were not going to mess around anymore. "I mean it, Jeff," she told him. "We're going to wait."

"He didn't like my announcement at all!" Gina says. "But I wanted to do what was right. And I'm so glad we did. It was definitely worth it."

Don't Just Say No

When Scott and I were in the heat of the moment, my saying no while my body was saying, "Yes. Yes, yes, yes, yes, oh yeah," was not the most effective way to maintain my decision to abstain from bodily pleasures.

The fact is, God made us to progress sexually. Kissing leads to necking, which leads to petting, which leads to heavy petting . . .

Those are all good things. Those are all ways God created us to enjoy each other. Sex is a good thing. But sex is specifically, exclusively, designed for couples who are married.

Now that I'm married, I see more clearly why God created it that way. He didn't put up that boundary to be harsh, to put a damper on our fun, or to be a moralistic prude. He did it for our good.

If you aren't a virgin, if you've been sexually active with your fiancé—or with anyone else—now's the time to make a fresh start. While you can't regain your virginity, you can start anew from this point with a clean slate. One of my favorite verses is Philippians 3:13: "I am focusing all my energies on this one thing: Forgetting the past and looking forward to what lies ahead."

As my friend Jennifer discovered, you can't just say, "We're not having sex." You need to be specific. Being intimate covers more than just copulating. Unfortunately, it's not a black-and-white issue. You know where that dangerous line is. That's the line you will need to agree to steer clear of.

Sharing Expectations and Setting Boundaries

The closer you get to the wedding, the more important it is to talk about sexual expectations with your fiancé. You probably won't want to talk about it when you're in the middle of a make-out session. Talk about it when you are sitting at the dinner table.

Esther did a smart thing before she and her fiancé, Dale, got married. She told him about her feelings regarding sex. "I let him know not to expect sex on our wedding night," she says. "I knew I'd be exhausted."

Just as couples need to communicate with each other about other areas to have a healthy marriage, we need to communicate about our sexual expectations too. This is an important conversation before you get married because it will affect your marital satisfaction and health for years. Let him know you need to go very, *very* slowly, for instance.

Jeane and her fiancé, Tyson, talked about exactly what would be acceptable and what wouldn't be. "We did a lot of making out during that time," Jeane says. "We had a neck-only rule. He could kiss my neck—but that was as low as he could go." They also didn't allow themselves to be alone a lot. "We knew it would be really difficult, so we didn't allow ourselves to be in compromising positions or in places that would present opportunities."

Sometimes it has to be an abrupt departure. "I'd say, 'Okay, I gotta go now. See ya,'" says one bride. She also asked an accountability partner to ask her the tough questions to keep her on track. You don't want to give a part of you to someone—even your fiancé—that you can never take back.

Be specific when you discuss your boundaries and expectations. My friend Jennifer went so far as to write up a formal contract with her fiancé, Brian. In it, she specified what was appropriate and what wasn't. For instance, they could take a nap together—but only with the door open. Brian was allowed to hold her hands and touch her arms, but he wasn't allowed to touch her below the shoulders. They could kiss but not for a long period of time. When she told me about their contract, I thought, *That's overdoing it a bit, don't you think?* That was, of course, before I started to date Scott seriously. And once we got engaged, forget it. I realized she might have been onto something.

I recommend talking about sexual expectations before marriage with one caveat: Be careful where and when you discuss it, because believe it or not, talking about making love is, in a sense, foreplay. Even talking about not having it makes you want to have it!

Get God Involved

The best way to start fresh is to talk to God about your past experiences. He already knows, but he's waiting for you to admit they were wrong choices. Ask him to forgive you of those wrong choices. He will! He'll lift them off you, and you'll feel free and clean, like a huge weight was taken from your soul.

The most amazing thing is that God is a God of grace. He won't condemn you. The Bible says that once you've dealt honestly with your wrong choices and actions before God, he will not only forgive you, he will no longer keep a record of them. Psalm 103:12 says, "He has removed our rebellious acts as far away from us as the east is from the west." And Hebrews 8:12 tells us that God says, "I will forgive their wrongdoings, and I will never again remember their sins." That's an awesome promise.

Past Negative Sexual Experiences

There is this sad, horrific reality that in this world there is evil. And many times evil happens to us through betrayal by someone we trust. I know a family whose father sexually abused his three daughters. The mother knew about it and chose not to prosecute. The secret finally came out when one of the daughters had a nervous breakdown. The father's evil actions have since become a curse on the family, causing divorce, infidelity, and pain to run rampant after the daughters married.

If you've been sexually abused or date raped, read this carefully: *What happened to you was not your fault.* You didn't deserve it, nor did you "ask for it." But you will want to get some professional help before you get married, because those experiences that were cruelly and unjustly pushed on you will affect your sex life with your husband. Sex between two married people is so pure and beautiful that it needs to be safeguarded and protected. There are several resources that can help you so that your past negative experiences don't mar the beauty of your marriage relationship. Remember, you're getting better, you're healing, and that's nothing to be ashamed of.

The book *Beauty Restored* by Me Ra Koh is a great resource for you to check out.[7] The author shares her experience and healing from date rape. She's honest and vulnerable about how it affected her relationship with her husband. You can also contact the American Association of Christian Counselors (www.aacc.net) or The American Association of Pastoral Counselors (www.aapc.org) to find a Christian counselor in your area.

Outside Sex Sources

Your fiancé may be a nice guy, he may seem strong in his spiritual life, and he may also be into pornography. This is one discussion that is important to have before you get married.

Ask him how he feels about looking at pornography. Does he see anything wrong with viewing *Playboy* or racy Internet sites? Has he ever called a 900 number or seen an X-rated movie? His answer will be telling. He may enjoy partaking in that and may not see anything wrong with it.

Stacey found this to be true. The only problem was she didn't find out until after she and Mike married. "It's devastating to my self-esteem!" says Stacey. "I wish I would have asked him about it before we were married so I could have dealt with it then."

Just as men need to be aware of the dangers pornography can bring into marriage, women also can be tempted. Online chat rooms and racy romance novels or anything that causes you to fantasize about anyone other than your spouse is direct disobedience to God. In the Old Testament Book of Job, Job says, "I made a covenant with my eyes not to look with lust upon a young woman" (31:1). And the writer of Proverbs tells us, "Above all else, guard your heart, for it affects everything you do" (4:23). The apostle Paul writes in Romans 6:12–13:

> Do not let sin control the way you live; do not give in to its lustful desires. Do not let any part of your body become a tool of wickedness, to be used for sinning. Instead, give yourselves completely to God since you have been given new life. And use your whole body as a tool to do what is right for the glory of God.

You will want to take care of any outside sex sources before you get married. While they may seem harmless, they can grow into something that will destroy your marriage.

Other Important Discussions

There are two more talks you'll want to have with your fiancé before you get married: choosing birth control and understanding PMS.

Birth Control Options: My engaged roommate, Amy, and I were driving home from play rehearsal when she whipped out this box. "I went to my gynecologist today," she said. "I decided on a type of birth control." Then she showed me this small round rubber thing. "What is it?" I asked. "It's a diaphragm," she said.

"And you put that where exactly?" I asked incredulously. I couldn't comprehend filling that with lubricating jelly and sticking it in my vagina. One look at that made me realize that it wasn't the direction I wanted to go with my birth control selection. Plus you have to take it out and clean it. "But what if you want to have sex after you take it out?" That was in my premarriage days when I thought Scott and I would have sex seventeen times in one night—every night. "Um, you use a condom, I guess," was Amy's expert reply.

Even though you and your fiancé have agreed to abstain from having sex until after the wedding, the two of you need to plan which method you want to practice when the time comes. I assume you are going to use some sort of birth control. I'm not going to go into which is best—that's something you need to identify for yourself with the help of your gynecologist.

Before you get married, you need to visit your gynecologist for a physical—including the dreaded Pap smear. While you're there, your doctor can give you a complete rundown on the different types of birth control and how they work. You may also consider reading a Christian book on the subject. *Birth Control for Christians* by Jenell Williams Paris explores both the physical practicalities and moral decisions involved in choosing between the various methods.

I'd also recommend discussing the different options with close friends or family members with whom you feel comfortable. While your gynecologist can give you the medical information, your girlfriends can give you the practical lowdown and the pros and cons. The better informed you are and the more you discuss it with your fiancé, the better decision you and your fiancé will be able to make.

105

PMS: One of the best things you can do for your marriage before you wed is to talk to your fiancé about your menstrual cycle. This may feel uncomfortable for you—and more than likely it will be awkward for him!—but let's face it, you won't be able to hide it from him after you're married like you can before you're married.

Scott and I talked about what happens to me every month. How I feel, how I want to be treated, how he shouldn't take my outbursts personally. He figured it out quickly when I lost my sense of humor or when I'd cry at a McDonald's commercial.

Because men don't experience the "joys" of "that time of the month," they're pretty clueless about what to do. Be gentle. Even if he's been reared in a family full of women, this is a different situation for him—you're his fiancé, not his sister or his mother. He expects his sisters to be rude and obnoxious. It baffles him, however, when his fiancé is.

If you're marrying a man who has been married before, the same advice applies. He may have lived with another woman as his wife, but he's never lived with *you*. And you are different than his other "women."

Final Words

Regardless of where you stand in the sexual department, here are a few words from the Bible to keep in mind as you wait to give your body to your husband:

> Look straight ahead, and fix your eyes on what lies before you. Mark out a straight path for your feet; then stick to the path and stay safe. Don't get sidetracked; keep your feet [body] from following evil.
>
> Proverbs 4:25–27

> Forget the former things;
> do not dwell on the past.

See, I am doing a new thing!
Now it springs up; do you not perceive it?
I am making a way in the desert
and streams in the wasteland.

Isaiah 43:18–19 NIV

— Quick Tips —

Want to avoid sex? Just show your fiancé your seventh grade school photo—or you look at his!

Eileen, married two years

Ask someone—not your fiancé—to hold you accountable. Have them ask you the tough questions—such as, "Are you two becoming too intimate?" You'll be grateful you did.

Jeane, married four years

Keep imagining the romance of your honeymoon night and how special that time will be. Save yourself for that occasion.

Madelyn, married two years

— Quick Quips —

Sex is never an emergency.

Elaine Pierson, physician

A kiss can be a comma, a question mark, or an exclamation point. That's basic punctuation every woman ought to know.

Mistinguette, French entertainer

Part 2

Your Wedding

NINE

"AAAAAhhhhh! I Need One More Day!"

The clock is ticking down! And if you haven't yet passed out from the panic of still needing to cross off things from your to-do list, take heart, the day hasn't ended yet.

No matter the length of your engagement period, you will still have things you need to finish before you're ready to walk down the aisle. I know — I seriously considered postponing my wedding for another week.

This is the time to let things go. Unless you plan to wear an extra thick veil on your wedding day, it's not worth the bags under the eyes, the cold sores and eczema, the diarrhea, the acne.

Avoiding Last Minute Stress

The week before the wedding is going to be chaotic. You'll have final appointments to attend, and your out-of-town guests will begin arriving. How do you get everything done?

A former coworker of mine, Chris, battled this dilemma in an interesting way. When she and her fiancé, Jerry, set the wedding for a Saturday, she pretended her wedding was actually on the Wednesday before that Saturday. "I decided that whatever wasn't finished by Wednesday I wasn't going to worry about," Chris says, "other than actually decorating the church and having the florist come. That way I had the last few days to relax and spend time with my family. I gave myself permission not to worry about the things that didn't get finished."

The best thing is to use this final week to pack for your honeymoon, wrap the attendants' gifts, and put a hold on your mail and newspapers or forward them to your new residence. Also, write out the checks for the people you'll pay on the wedding day (the officiant, the musicians . . .) and have those ready to go so you don't have to worry about that the week — or day! — of the wedding.

This is also a good time to put together a wedding day emergency kit. Make up the kit and give it to your coordinator or a friend or family member who's close to you. It may include extra cosmetics, extra hosiery, an antacid or peppermints (peppermints are great for an upset stomach), adhesive bandages (for blisters or cuts), hairspray, tissues, breath mints (or if you like lemon drops, those work well too), eye drops (especially if you wear contacts), safety pins, deodorant, bottled water, and stain remover.

Worrisome What-Ifs

"What do you mean the pastor fell and hit his head?" said a panicked Carol when a groomsman relayed the news. Less than ten minutes before the ceremony was to begin, the minister fell, hit his head on the side of a table, and needed stitches. Fortunately, he was good-natured about it. He cleaned his wound, put a bandage on it, and went on with the ceremony. Then afterward, one of the ushers drove him to the hospital.

"We were concerned he was going to pass out in the middle of the wedding vows!" her husband, Sam, says.

We've all heard about brides—and even grooms—who have fainted during a wedding ceremony. Recently I attended my cousin Jennifer's outdoor, over 100-degree wedding, in which her maid of honor was stung by a bee and passed out.

Obviously, if you plan to have an outdoor wedding, you will want to consider alternatives in the case of rain, sleet, freak snowstorms, floods, hurricanes, tornadoes. There are just some things that are out of your influence. Someone once said, "Don't allow your happiness to be based on things we can't control, which is, basically, everything."

Let's face it, you cannot be prepared for every possible worst-case scenario. Fires, accidents, plane crashes, tripping down the aisle, hiccupping, PMS, the flu. One of my worst-case scenarios was wondering what toast my brother-in-law was going to give.

My friend Amy's wedding dress was misdelivered to a law firm in St. Louis—two states away and two days before the wedding. Did she worry? You bet. Did it help the situation? No. The dress eventually arrived at the local Feed & Sack store (who knows why there?), and everything turned out fine, but not because she worried about it.

About three weeks before my wedding, I started to have nightmares. I would wake in a cold sweat because I had dreamt the reception hall had three different groups in it when it was just supposed to be my reception, or that I'd done all this work and no one came to the wedding. And the dreams felt so real.

So what can you do when something happens over which you have no control? Simply ask yourself, *Will this really make a difference in five years? Ten years? In the light of eternity?* If not, give yourself a pep talk and say, *It's okay. It's not the end of the world.*

Sometimes worries turn out to be blessings in disguise. For instance, a few weeks before my wedding, when I contacted the reception hall coordinator to ask a question, as an afterthought she mentioned they had booked a breakfast banquet in my reception room on my wedding day, which meant I couldn't get in the day before or the day of the wedding to decorate. That announcement sent me whirling into worry over what the condition of the hall would be like. Would there be scraps of food all over the floor? Would the tables be decorated correctly? But the restaurant's employees decorated the entire hall beautifully — and for free.

The Neglected Fiancé

The day of the rehearsal, I was frazzled with all of the running around trying to put finishing touches on everything. We rushed to the rehearsal, then to the rehearsal dinner, and everything seemed to be a blur — until I noticed Scott was acting standoffish. I had been so busy making sure everything was just right, I had neglected to look after him.

Finally, after the rehearsal dinner, Scott commented, "It would be nice if I could spend some time with my bride-to-be." Ouch. What was I doing? Here was the love of my life, and I was neglecting him.

Susan discovered she was doing this too. After the rehearsal, her fiancé, David, asked her if they could spend some private time together. "Can we have just fifteen minutes together?"

"I really didn't have the time," says Susan. "My sister and I were wrapping the wedding party gifts!" But she asked her sister to finish them so she could spend a few moments alone with David. "It's a good thing I did," says Susan. "He wanted to give me a present and tell me how much he loved me. If I hadn't taken that time, I would have missed a beautiful blessing from him."

Whenever my parents would visit Scott and me, my mother would say, "No matter who is around, you pay attention to your man first and foremost. Men need that reassurance."

Between all the details, planning, and organizing, your fiancé may feel as if he's part of your to-do list — if he even makes the list. Try to carve out time to spend with him — time in which you don't even mention the wedding. Enjoy him. After all, once the wedding is over, he'll still be in the picture.

The Neglected Bride

The day before and the day of your wedding, you will be surrounded by people. As one bride says, "Everyone wants a piece of you!" After all, everything is centered around you, the bride. But what about you? You need some time alone — even just ten minutes can make a difference.

I rose early the day of my wedding and soaked in the bathtub. It was relaxing, and it allowed me an opportunity to clear my thoughts and pamper myself. It's vital — especially if you're an introvert. If it's in your budget, pamper yourself with a massage. Or take a long, hot shower. Try to spend some "me" time with yourself. You don't have to feel guilty about it. Take a walk during which you do not allow yourself to think about the wedding. Concentrate on your breathing. Look at nature. Worship God for his creativity. Sing as many songs from *The Sound of Music* or *Mary Poppins* as you can remember. Find a playground and swing. Go to a pond and feed the ducks. Just take a few moments to be alone with yourself.

Dedicate Your Marriage to God

Before our wedding, Scott and I did something I'll treasure forever. It's also something I look back on to remind me of my commitment.

After the rehearsal and the rehearsal dinner, Scott and I, along with my parents, returned to the church and, kneeling at the altar, presented our married life to God.

Countdown Surprises for Your Spouse

Want a way to build extra excitement for the wedding day? Give your fiancé special presents each day the week of your wedding. If you're unable to do that, give him the presents starting from the rehearsal right up through the wedding! Here are a few tips to get you started.

• If you and your fiancé wrote love e-mails to each other during your courtship, now's the time to print them — presuming you saved them — and paste them in a book. Present the book to him during some private time after the rehearsal.

• Call his favorite radio station and dedicate "your" song to him. Make sure he tunes in!

• Write him a silly poem: "Roses are red, violets are blue, in a few hours, I'll be married to you!" Or you can write him something more serious.

• The day of the wedding, hand a groomsman a stack of greeting cards to deliver to your sweetie at the top of each hour leading up to the ceremony.

• Do something during the ceremony or reception he's not expecting (shoving cake in his face is not recommended). I surprised my groom by singing a song to him at our reception. He loved it!

We asked God to be a special guest at our wedding ceremony and the reception. We asked him to bless our union and to help us always remember our wedding day with the promise and hope it held for a committed future.

Obviously we were in a special situation since my dad was the minister of that church. But you can do this easily. Ask the pastor to allow you some time to pray and invite him to pray over you as well. If you're not getting married in a church, find a special place where you can spend time together praying for God to join you in the festivities. If you have issues you need to work through in your relationship with God, do your marriage a favor and still invite him to the wedding. Make your wedding bigger than just you and your fiancé. God yearns to be part of your life. And he will give you one of the best wedding gifts you will receive — namely, his blessing on your marriage.

— Quick Tips —

Determine what your ceremony will include — before the rehearsal. I was involved in one wedding in which the bride and groom spent most of the rehearsal trying to decide what they wanted to have happen during the ceremony.

Madelyn, married two years

Avoid having a bachelorette party or bridal shower the night before your wedding. You'll feel rushed, stressed, and glazed over, and you may not enjoy it as much.

Eileen, married two years

If during these last few days you find yourself losing your sense of humor, rent *My Big Fat Greek Wedding* and watch it. I'm sure you won't have a wedding like that, and it will put everything in perspective.

Madelyn, married two years

Ten

Last Moments of Being Nearly-Wed

I t's Murphy's Law: You plan for something important and perfect, and something or someone somewhere will not cooperate. The Acu-Weather Five Day Forecast is a perfect example.

The good news is that your wedding day will probably not be nearly as exciting as Donna and John's wedding day. First Donna backed her bridesmaid's car into a passing van when she arrived at the site where they were taking their wedding photos before the ceremony. Then before the ceremony, unbeknownst to her, she cut her finger and bled on her wedding gown. During the ceremony John and Donna were going to sing a duet to each other, but John's microphone wire tangled, which flustered him into singing Donna's verse. Donna was puzzled but then sang John's verse to him, which flustered John so much he turned his back on her and grabbed the music "cheat sheet," which forced Donna to sing to her fiancé's back.

At the reception hall the electricity went out — and remained out for several hours. To compensate for the lack of light, some friends parked their cars toward the windows and turned on their headlights, while other friends went to Home Depot and bought a portable generator so they could run their sound system and slide show. Of course, right before the slide show ended the lights came on, and they had to run and turn them off.

That night, John and Donna missed their flight because Donna misplaced her I.D. They ended up taking a red-eye flight that night from San Francisco, got ill, and both ended up in a New Hampshire hospital. Maybe it wasn't a romantic time, but it was certainly memorable.

Whether it's a small snafu or a huge hang-up, one guarantee is that your wedding day will not be flawless. You can do everything Martha Stewart and all the etiquette books suggest and still have something you did not plan for happen. But, says one bride, "you can make your wedding day *seem* perfect. Everyone is going to take his or her cue from you. If you are calm, they will be too."

Before You Leave Your House

As I was growing up, whenever my family would take vacations, my mom would stop us before we left and say, "Let's go through everything. Did you pack your deodorant? Did you pack the tickets? Do you have extra film? Your toothbrush? Your contact solution?" She would talk us through whatever we would need for the trip. It saved us a lot of heartache when she would help us discover we had forgotten something. We were able to retrieve the item before we even got in the car.

The same applies for what you'll take to the ceremony the day of the wedding. Talk it through with someone, perhaps your mother or your wedding coordinator, before you leave your house.

The night before my best friend's wedding, we laughed and stayed up talking until around 1:00 A.M. Then we headed to her room to try to sleep. We'd just started to doze, when a loud "Oh, shoot!" came from the living room. My friend was up in an instant and headed into the living room where her mother and sister were. Her mother had forgotten to make the wedding veil. Her mom stayed up most of the night sewing the veil—only to leave it at the house when they left for the church.

The Waiting Game: Dressing Too Early

I noticed something interesting about the weddings I was in before I got married. The brides were ready long before the ceremony began. I was even surprised that my wedding was like that. I remember at my friend Amy's wedding she kept saying, "Could we just turn all the clocks ahead? I'm ready to go! Let's get this show on the road."

If this happens to you, there are two directions you can go: One is to focus on the imperfections of the day. One bride, Betsey, dressed too early. "That was a big mistake," says Betsey. "I was ready way too soon and was just standing around. I didn't know what to do with myself, and so I started to notice what wasn't perfect, like the fact that the florist hadn't arrived yet."[1] It gave her

Did You Know?

In a 2002 *Ladies' Home Journal* poll:

55 percent of respondents said their wedding day was the happiest day of their lives

12 percent said they were so tense on their wedding day that they couldn't enjoy it

33 percent said that if they could change one thing about their wedding, they would have invited more guests

something to worry about, which is exactly what she didn't need to do on her wedding day.

The other direction is to take those few remaining moments to voice your gratitude to special people. Ask your coordinator to summon your grandmother or a favorite aunt or your mom and dad. Gather your bridesmaids and thank them for being in your life. Tell them how much you appreciate their support and their sharing this time with you.

What Do You Mean, It's Not about Me?

At a work-related event several years ago, I heard a well-known minister say, "Weddings aren't really about the bride." I remember thinking, *Yeah, right.* After all, who plans the whole thing? For whom does the congregation stand? The groom? I don't think so. What march is played? "The Wedding Party March"? "Here Come the Bridesmaids"? No. It's "Here Comes the Bride."

Then I got married and discovered the minister was correct. The wedding isn't about the bride. We brides think it is; everyone says it is. But it isn't. It's also a lot of other people's day. It's your family's day. It's your friends' day. The wedding is about everyone involved. Parents, family, children, bridesmaids, friends, acquaintances, church members . . .

Even though you and your fiancé are in the spotlight, everyone there has a stake in your wedding's success or failure. Everyone brings with them their hopes, dreams, and baggage. Their desires are riding on you—that you'll succeed, that you'll beat the odds, that you'll be happy. To a certain extent, if your wedding is a success, those people will also be a success.

With this realization, I felt calmer, and I expanded my focus to include everyone.

Laughter: That Which Cures All Things

My mom and I had a running joke throughout my engagement that I was the little princess. One day while I was shopping, I found some tissues that had "I'm a princess" etched on them. So I bought them, thinking I'd pass one to her on my wedding day. Sure enough, that morning I nonchalantly placed one in her hand. She took one look and started laughing. That was such a bonding—and calming—moment for us.

Laughter helped me through the stressful times during my engagement and wedding day. For instance, one of the funniest moments was when my matron of honor, Amy, started walking around in front of me like Charlie Chaplin before the wedding.

When I was a bridesmaid at a friend's wedding, we were ready early and waiting for the ceremony to begin. The problem was that the bride's mother was a nervous wreck. Finally, the bride came to me and said, "Ginger, would you go tell my mother a joke? She just needs to laugh. If she doesn't laugh, I'm afraid she's going to have a nervous breakdown—and take me with her."

Look for something to laugh about. It helps you refocus and not take everything so seriously. Laughter is healthy and is a great cure for any imperfections on your wedding day.

—Quick Tips—

Make sure you wear waterproof mascara!

Eileen, married two years

If you have an aisle runner, make sure it's tacked down. Otherwise, the weight of your dress swooshing across it may move it. Or if your wedding is outside, the wind may lift it. And you don't want to have to run after your runner.

> Madelyn, married two years

Try lightly spraying perfume in your hair. You'll smell great for hours!

> Amy, married five years

Make sure you have breakfast! Even if it's an energy bar or a glass of orange juice. You'll need it.

> Esther, married one year

If you're videotaping the ceremony, consider videotaping beforehand too while you're getting ready. That's a wonderful time you won't want to forget.

> Jeane, married four years

Make sure to communicate to your wedding day coordinator what you need her to do. I asked my fiancé's sister to act as my coordinator. She agreed, then didn't follow through! Thank goodness I didn't have a real emergency.

> Madelyn, married three years

— Quick Quips —

I was crushed when my ill father was unable to make it to my wedding. That brought everything into perspective for me. I had become bogged down with all the typical wedding stuff and lost the big picture. My father's illness caused me to

come back to center, to simplify many things. I
realized it's really not about a wedding; it's about
a marriage and relationships. The people are
always the only thing that truly matter.

Rachael, married three months

After the ceremony we decided to go out for a
spin in the convertible, then head over to the
party. It was about 6:00 P.M., and we were all
dressed up, driving around in this outrageous
car with the videographers following us just like
paparazzi. We attracted a lot of attention and
were honking and waving at everyone, which was
great fun. Then we decided to have some burgers
and fries, just in case we didn't have time to eat
later, and went through the drive-through at
McDonald's.[2]

Betsey, married two years

Eleven

Walking the Aisle

Bliss. Pure, simple, unadulterated bliss. That's one of the most wonderful emotions you can expect to have wash over you this day. It doesn't matter that you haven't slept in weeks, your nerves are shot, and you discovered your photographer called in sick. When you walk down that aisle, you will be overcome with the joy of the moment and what it represents.

Welcome to your wedding day. It's the Big Day—capital B, capital D. This is one of the few occasions that will reflect your values, beliefs, traditions, and tastes. And it should. "I've been to so many weddings where the ceremony was cookie cutter," one bride says. "I left without any sense of the personality of the couple. On the other hand, at my brother-in-law's reception, he and his new bride entered the reception hall wearing these cheesy Dallas Cowboys plastic helmets. Well, they might have been cheesy, but that was so them! And I loved it because of that."

This is also the day that may seem disorganized and surreal. That's okay. Time has a way of organizing and drifting you along. Today all the guests are seated and waiting, the groom is in the building, and the processional has started. It's time to kick back and enjoy the day you've been planning and looking forward to for, well, your whole life.

Be in the Moment

The day of your wedding will be surreal, as if you are walking through a dream. Throughout Amy's wedding day, her sister, Shelley, forced Amy to stop and take everything in. "We all thought Shelley was a loon because she kept saying, 'Amy, stop. Just stop and remember this moment,'" Amy says. "She did it as we were leaving the house to go to the church. She did it when I was putting on my dress. She made Todd and me stop and look, really look, at the wedding cake. But you know what? Those are the moments I remember clearly. Everything else is a blur — but I remember those moments with my sister! And I'm so glad she gave me that gift."

There are special moments I remember clearly: Sharing orange juice and half a Xanax with my mother at 5:45 A.M.; hugging my father before we entered the sanctuary; looking into my fiancé's eyes for the first time that day. Another one was spending time with people who traveled many miles to share my day, one of whom I'll never see again this side of heaven. The brief moments I had with my Uncle Holly at the wedding and reception were my last with him — he died four months later. And I will cherish those moments forever.

On your wedding day make sure you stop and seize moments to take everything in. Don't get lost in the busyness of dealing with the dress and your hair and the ring bearer's tantrums. You'll never have this opportunity again. Make a special effort to freeze-frame specific things about your day.

Intentional Moments
with Special People

How can you take everything in? People who have known you for your entire life surround you. "My mind couldn't comprehend the fact that people were so kind and loved me so much," says one bride. Special moments with people will be branded in your memory when you make them intentional. When I stood in the kitchen and drank orange juice with my mother, we didn't express our unending loyalty to each other. To be honest, the moment probably didn't have the meaning to my mom that it did to me. But just to be able to do something so simple with her was a treasure I still prize. I thanked her for bringing me to this day and for all she did. And I told her I loved her. It's that simple.

I was able to do that as well with my dad right before we walked down the aisle. We hugged and told each other a joke so neither of us would cry. We used our special nicknames for each other. Again, it was only a few moments, but those moments were precious.

Once you walk down that aisle, you won't have as many opportunities to be intentional, because everything will wind up and start rolling along at a pace you'll hardly be able to keep up with. So find those few moments to tell the people who mean the most to you how you feel about them. A simple "thank you" and "I love you" do remarkable things—to both the giver and the receiver.

Looking for the Unexpected

We were missing an important person at our wedding: Scott's dad, Ed. Ed had passed away unexpectedly nine months before our ceremony. He never lived to see me join the Kolbaba gang. I knew it would be disappointing for Scott and his family not to have their father be part of this celebration. So when we visited the florist, I asked her to create a special bouquet to place near the altar in dedication to Ed. Since Ed's favorite color was orange, I also asked the florist to add some orange flowers. She cringed. "Orange won't match anything in your color scheme," she said. "I'll tell you what, how about we put a few orange flowers in the back of the bouquet?" I agreed and didn't think about it again until right after the ceremony. We were shooting our photos on the stage when I glanced toward the flowers. They were sitting next to a stained glass window, and the sun was beaming through the window, shining on the bouquet. The glass was orange, which gave an orange tint to the flowers.

As I looked over, my breath caught in my throat. Then I gently tapped Scott and pointed to the bouquet of now orange flowers. He was quiet for a moment as we realized God had presented us with a wonderful blessing. It was as though he was reassuring us that Ed was looking down and smiling. What a special wedding gift.

Another bride, Amy, also had an unexpected present, this one from her new grandmother-in-law. As the recessional music played and the new Mr. and Mrs. Derrick Todd Bell walked down the aisle, Todd's grandmother stepped out into the aisle right in front of the couple, grabbed Amy's hand, shoved something in it, clasped it tightly, and said, "This is for groceries, you're going to need it." When Amy got to the back of the church she looked at her hand. She was holding a $50 bill. "That was one of my favorite, and funniest, memories," Amy says. "It was certainly unexpected!"

When Someone Isn't "With the Program"

Normally you don't expect a minister to flub up your wedding. He's the professional, after all. But Mark and Nina discovered that ministers can be human too.

Mark and Nina had planned to take communion during the ceremony and then serve it to their guests. The problem was that the minister, who was in charge of preparing communion, forgot to bring the essentials: the bread and wine. The other problem was that no one realized his oversight, including the minister himself, until that point in the ceremony. As Mark and Nina knelt at the altar, the minister approached the communion table and said loudly, "Oh my. Friends, I've made a mistake." Mark and Nina wanted just to move on to the next thing in the ceremony. But the minister leaned forward and said, "I have an idea. Trust me."

"No," said Mark. But the minister proceeded to serve the pretend communion to Mark and Nina, then announced that they would hold the imaginary bread and wine for the guests to partake. So Mark and Nina served the "bread" and "wine" as the entire audience of about three hundred people mimicked taking communion. "What else could we do?" Mark says. "We did it and laughed through the entire thing. We had to laugh—how could we take that seriously?"

Another bride could only laugh as well when her fiancé's brother read an Old Testament passage from the Bible during the ceremony. Since many of the guests were from out of town, the couple had decided to keep the rehearsal brief, so the readers were told when to read but didn't actually rehearse it the night before. That was unfortunate, since the groom's brother, being nervous, kept pronouncing the biblical term Yahweh as "Yahoo." By the third Yahoo, the congregation was laughing out loud.

But what about those times that aren't funny? For instance, Jennifer's mom wouldn't speak to her the day of the wedding, and before the photos were taken, her mom disappeared. After they searched everywhere for her, they finally found her across the street at Jennifer's house, watching CNN, drinking coffee, and smoking a cigarette.

"I don't remember a lot of sentimentality that day," admits Jennifer. "But I did get a note from my sister that had beautiful things written in it. She knew our mother wouldn't do that." How did Jennifer deal with her mother? "I refused to think about it. I knew if I allowed myself to dwell on her actions, I could get extremely hurt. So I chose not to. I chose to enjoy my day."

Guests

One word on guests: I officially give you permission not to worry about them. They'll take care of themselves. Feel free to focus on you and your new spouse and enjoy yourselves. This is one thing I wish I had done differently.

I had attended too many weddings where the guests sat at the reception with nothing to do and nothing to eat waiting for the bridal couple to arrive, so I told Scott, "For our wedding we're starting the reception on time. I don't want our guests to have to wait." I admire my thoughtfulness for the guests, but it really wasn't necessary. We were running late with our photo session, and because we wanted to get there "on time," we were unable to take a lot of photos we wanted. Plus I missed spending more time alone with my new spouse. We were too busy rushing!

Of course, I'm not suggesting you don't think at all about your guests, but don't allow their comfort to be your over-riding concern. If you run late, you run late. Enjoy that time without worrying about whether or not your guests are going to be irritated. They probably won't remember anyway. And if they do, I'm sure they'll get over it eventually.

It's All in the Attitude

My nephew Buzz and his bride-to-be, Sarah, had planned for their wedding and reception to take place at a lovely banquet hall. The problem was there was another wedding reception that would also be taking place. The weddings would be separated by a partition. Sarah and Buzz had made sure the other wedding party's reception would begin *after* their wedding ceremony was finished. No problem, they were promised. And that seemed to be the case—until their ceremony got started a half-hour late. The ceremony began. Sarah was, of course, beautiful. The hall was decorated lavishly. The guests were seated in anticipation of a touching and romantic wedding. And so it was—until the vows.

Sarah and Buzz had written their vows, and they began to recite them precisely when the reception next door got under way. As Sarah and Buzz spoke the vows they'd spent long nights writing, the vows they had painstakingly memorized and were now nervously sharing, the deejay next door played the theme from *Rocky*. Loudly.

Fun Reception Ideas

- Hire professional magicians to perform before the reception to entertain the guests.
- Tell the story of your romance. Authors Cynthia Rowley and Ilene Rosenzweig offer this idea: Assign a dozen of your friends and family members to make a toast. Each one will tell a chapter of your romance—from the moment you met to the "ring-a-ding day you got the rock." Each person can relate an anecdote, offer a show-and-tell item, or dress up and act out an event in your courtship (all clean, of course). Stagger the performances throughout the reception (toasts don't only have to be after dinner). Ring wedding bells to signal each one. After you cut the cake, take a group photo: Have those guests flip over their plates and lift them overhead. On the bottom of each is a letter that spells out, "And they lived happily ever after."[1]
- Be spontaneous. Tradition states that when the guests clank on their glasses, the bride and groom kiss. No wonder you don't get a chance to eat! At our reception, we turned the tables when Scott leaned over to me and suggested he and I clang our glasses and make all the guests grab *their* sweeties and plant a kiss on them. That was great fun to watch.

Next the deejay announced each member of the wedding party—the large Italian wedding party. The music he chose this time was the theme to *Star Wars*.

We were unable to hear anything that took place during the ceremony, and I cringed when I realized that directly after the vows their vocalist was going to perform "From This Moment On."

What a disaster, I thought. During the reception everyone talked about how horrible they felt for Sarah and Buzz. Everyone agreed that they deserved to be upset and should complain to the management.

What I didn't expect was their attitude. I spoke with Sarah several weeks after the wedding and asked her about it. She said, "At the time, Buzz and I were crushed. But after we returned from the honeymoon, we took a look at the video. Yes, we heard the Rocky theme song during our vows. But we also realized that we were so tuned in to our purpose there and to each other that I look at our wedding as the most beautiful wedding I could have asked for—even with the disaster from next door."

If any bride had the right to be upset and devastated by the events that occurred during her ceremony, it was definitely Sarah. Yet her attitude allowed her to look at the ceremony as beautiful. And I have to agree. It was beautiful . . . and definitely unique.

I loved my wedding, and you'll love yours. And pretty much regardless of what happens (and believe me, something will), at the end of the day every wedding is perfect. Trust me on this: As long as you've signed that marriage certificate, your fiancé shows up and says "I do," and the officiant says, "I now pronounce you Mr. and Mrs. . . . ." you're married—and the wedding was perfect.

— Quick Tips —

Rethink having a bubble machine at your
reception. They are romantic — but cause slippery
dance floors!

H. Norman Wright,
married more than forty years

Decorate a box that's lockable as a place for
guests to put their gift cards. My friend had all
her cards — with all the money in them — stolen at
her reception.

Eileen, married two years

If you plan to recite your own vows, make sure
the officiant has a copy of them. That way, if you
forget to bring your copy, the officiant can loan
you his.

Scott, married three years

While guests are waiting to sign the guest
book or waiting to be seated, on a nearby table
place photos of you and your fiancé, as well as
photos of your parents, his parents, and all the
grandparents. It would be especially nice to
display their wedding photos on the table as well.
This way guests can see your heritage.

Kay, married three years

Instead of having your guests throw rice or
birdseed or blow bubbles at you or let helium
balloons go after the wedding, consider having
them pop "popper" firecrackers above your

head — the kind that have the colored streamers in them. Not the kind that ignite.

Ginger, married three years

Be prepared to hear the "So, when are you having kids?" questions. You'll get them — even before the wedding day!

Lisa, married three years

At our wedding, instead of the guests clinking glasses to see my husband and me kiss, we had them walk to the dance floor and work a hula hoop.

Amber, married one month

— Quick Quip —

In the February 2002 issue of *Glamour* magazine, author Stephanie Dolgoff gives two great pieces of advice regarding what no bride should worry about: (1) "Having Jordan almonds on the table. Nobody will say, 'Lovely wedding, but can you believe she forgot the nuts?'" and (2) "Looking klutzy during your first dance. Just gaga-gaze at each other and sway — guests will think you're both adorable."

Part 3

Your Honeymoon

Do
Not
Disturb

TWELVE

Fun Things to Do on Your Wedding Night

Not Tonight, Honey

Be honest, this night has crossed your mind at least once, if not a dozen times, while you were planning your wedding. It's supposed to be a night of romance and ecstasy. It's the mystery of love culminating in this evening of passion. But really, it's the culmination of wedding planning exhaustion.

You've just spent months focused on planning a "perfect" wedding and your stress level is at its peak, so don't be surprised if you're just too tired to want to be intimate, or, to steal a phrase from psychologist Kevin Leman, you may be too pooped to whoop. You may want just to cuddle with your new spouse. Or like Esther, you may just want to be left alone to sleep! "After the reception," says Esther, "we went back to our new condo to start unwrapping presents and fell asleep on the floor. I was so tired."

One of the great myths of the wedding night is that you will have sex. This night above all others probably carries the greatest expectation about passion. While that may be true in some cases, it's not a requirement. Some couples spend the first night just sleeping in the same bed to get used to each other.

One groom admits: "I love my wife, but after spending more than an hour figuring out exactly how to get her complicated dress off, I fell into bed and went to sleep."

You may be surprised to know that a lot of couples don't have sex on their wedding night. It's just one of many nights to have sex. You have the rest of your married life. So relax and sleep. If you don't have sex on your wedding night, you're okay. Your first time having sex as a married couple is special. Why rush it or not enjoy it because you're so exhausted? If you're just too tired and your husband is ready to go, tell him honestly how you feel. "Honey, I love you, and I'm so excited about sharing myself with you as your wife. That's why I want it to be special. How about if we rest tonight? Then when we're both ready, we'll be able to enjoy it." If, for some reason, your new husband isn't keen on waiting another night, suggest a compromise: "How about we nap a couple of hours, then . . . " Either way, you don't have to feel pressured because of some expectation that newly-wedded couples have to be newly-bedded couples on their wedding night.

Fear Factor

If you are a virgin, or even if you aren't, you may feel a sense of nervousness about your first time making love with your husband. One new bride, Emma, felt this fear: "I told my husband I was afraid, so we talked about it, which helped ease some of my fears."

It's understandable if you have some fear. After all, sex is messy, it may sometimes be uncomfortable, it's an adjustment, it's awkward, it's embarrassing, and it's not always orgasmic. Your bodies may make funny, swishy noises, and the act itself may seem rather animalistic.

There's also the possibility that your first married sexual encounter will be a bit of a letdown. "I didn't feel anything!" admits Carrie of her wedding night. If you and/or your husband are nervous, the romantic nature of the night can turn out to be a dud. The good news is that this night is just one of hundreds of thousands of nights to practice, and talking about your nervousness helps.

But also consider some of the rewards of marital sex. Sex with your husband for the first time is an amazingly emotional experience. You forge a bond with your mate in an intimate way with which nothing else compares. It's more than just the physical aspects. "I was surprised how overwhelmed emotionally I became," one bride admits. "This person knows me intimately and has seen me vulnerable. To know I'll have that forever with him is a freeing and wonderful realization. People take sex so lightly, but it's a beautifully emotional gift."

You will be closer to your husband, you'll feel a sense of awe and wonder that God could bond you with your spouse, and you'll feel safe. After our first time making love, I felt the most beautiful emotional and spiritual connection to Scott, and I still feel that.

Sex is a special gift God has given you and your husband to enjoy and celebrate. That's why marriage is for a lifetime—we get a lifetime of practice! So try not to pressure yourself to "get it right." Take it slowly, breathe, and guide your husband. You're permitted to touch him and talk to him. Take his hand and find the places on your body where his caress feels good. Allow yourself to be free to enjoy this precious gift.

Eight Myths—and Truths!—about Honeymoon Sex

1. *Myth:* Sex will be natural. *Truth:* It takes practice to have good sex. Sex is a learning process. That's why God put sex into marriage. Because you'll need lots of time to get it right.

2. *Myth:* Sex will be just like in the movies. *Truth:* When was the last time you saw a couple on the big screen have mussed hair, get entangled in the sheets, or not climax? No men in the movies have premature ejaculation. And the women can work all day, clean the house, take care of the kids, volunteer, give advice to the neighbors, save a dying man, and then be thrilled to please their husbands in bed.

3. *Myth:* We'll make love for hours. *Truth:* I have one word for that: quickies. You may start out your love life having sex for hours, but after about the second time you have sex, it will get quicker and quicker.

4. *Myth:* My husband will rip off my clothes, and we'll have wild orgasms. *Truth:* This sounds, uh, romantic, but who wants her spouse to ruin a perfectly good shirt? And as for the wild orgasms, well, sometimes sex will be . . . passionate. But wild? Probably not so much.

5. *Myth:* We'll both be in the mood at the same time. *Truth:* Just because hubby's feeling frisky doesn't mean you're going to be automatically interested. As sexual counselors Clifford and Joyce Penner write in *Getting Your Sex Life Off to a Great Start,* "Unfortunately, sexual desire is not 'contagious.' . . . Sexual drive is an appetite. Just as each of you will differ in your appetite for food—the amount you eat and when you eat—you will likely experience differences in your sexual appetites."[1] The addendum to this myth is that contrary to popular belief, men are not always in the mood.

6. *Myth:* We'll climax at the same time. *Truth:* This is probably my favorite. I think we've done this once. If you do, great. If you don't, no big deal. Why add the pressure of setting that goal?

7. *Myth:* My husband will know how to please me. *Truth:* While your hubby may know the mechanics of sex and he may think about sex a lot, he doesn't have some internal guidebook that directs his every move to bring you to a multiorgasmic experience. Your husband will want to please you, but he needs your help. A guiding hand, a guttural moan, a "yes," or a "that

feels so good when you do that" will go a long way toward helping him please you.

8. *Myth:* We'll cuddle afterward, fall asleep in each other's arms, or have deep intimate discussions. *Truth:* Kelly's husband, Jeff, likes to sleep right after they have sex—except when it's time to sleep, he doesn't want to be touched. No cuddling, snuggling, nestling. "His idea of cuddling after sex is, 'Here's my side, there's yours. Use it,'" says Kelly. The other thing the media never reveals is that when those couples in the movies are wrapped in each other's arms, those arms are probably going from tingly to numb. How many movies have you watched where the man whispers, "Honey, I love this. Now move, my arm is asleep"?

A Sensual Surprise: Sex Is Messy

This was a personal shocker to me. Call me slow or naïve, but honestly, I thought sex was a clean activity. Hollywood never shows the romantic love scene with the candles, perfect lighting, soft music, and a towel for the cleanup afterward. "Media gives us a different picture," says Jennifer, a new bride. "Those people roll over and go to sleep. I roll over and take a shower!"

Not until a week before my wedding, when my mom and I were talking about what to expect on the wedding night, did she announce, "You know, it's messy." No, I didn't. At thirty-two years old, I didn't have a clue!

Your Sex Basket

After Jeane, a bride of four years, got married, she started to make honeymoon baskets for her close friends.

You may want to put one together for your honeymoon. It includes lubricant, feminine towelettes, mints, candles and matches, fancy air freshener from Bath & Body Works, and aspirin.

141

I had always thought about the romance of intimacy, not the mechanics of sex. Sex is untidy, slippery, sticky, sweaty. There are semen and vaginal secretions, funny faces, and guttural sounds. There may even be some seepage. It is not romantic. Romance comes before the act. The romance of married sex is when your husband reaches over and grabs your breast.

To enjoy sex completely, give yourself permission to abandon your physical inhibitions. In his book *A Celebration of Sex for Newlyweds,* Dr. Douglas Rosenau says,

> Being sensual, passionate, and playful is never neat. Bodies and their functions are never totally romantic, but they can create some marvelous sexual connection. It won't happen overnight, but active thrusting, sweat, semen, and vaginal secretions will become arousing stimulants of pleasure and sexual excitement as you associate them with your mate and fun times together.[2]

Here are some tips to deal with the untidiness of love-making.

- Try not to say such things as, "Eew! Gross. You're so messy!" These comments will not only destroy the intimacy of the moment, but they will devastate your husband. Remember, your husband wants to please you, and underneath the tough guy exterior is a little boy who has just shown his vulnerability. If you say, "Gross!" his insecurity could hit him hard, and you'll miss out on a wonderful opportunity to share your new bond.
- Keep a "sex" towel on hand. One gal I interviewed shared that she and her husband use a special towel for cleanup afterward. They keep it under the bed and bring it out whenever they have sex.
- Keep a box of tissues by the bed.
- Take a shower. Why not bond with your husband and take it together? You could even clean each other.

- Use a warm washcloth or feminine towelettes. Don't forget to clean off your husband too! That act of loving service will build your intimacy with him.

Sex Rules

What's okay and not okay in the bedroom? Is oral sex acceptable? What about sex toys or sex videos? Can I striptease for my husband? In my work as managing editor of *Marriage Partnership* magazine, I'm inundated with letters from couples who want to know what's allowable and healthy in a sexual relationship.

Keep in mind a few things that will enable you to enjoy fully your sexual experience with your husband. First, in *A Celebration of Sex*, Dr. Douglas Rosenau says this about sex: "In a great marriage, mates need to build an assertive responsible selfishness. Orgasm is a great example of Christian selfishness."[3] In other words, it's okay for you to give — *and receive* — pleasure. There's no reason for you to feel guilty or ashamed if you work to please yourself during sex.

However, there are also some boundaries you may want to keep in mind. God created you with the power to give and to receive intense pleasure. But he also established boundaries to protect the relationship you and your husband will have.

Marriage Partnership magazine's Real Sex columnists, Melissa McBurney and Louis McBurney, M.D., discuss the criteria for what to consider when wanting to try new things. In their column they list the three cardinal rules for lovemaking.

Mutuality. In other words, both of you must agree. Most couples will have different sexual interests ranging from frequency to positions to experimentation. In a *Marriage Partnership* article, "Christian Sex Rules," the McBurneys write, "This creates enormous opportunity for a couple to develop mutual submissiveness in their relationship. Each individual will have ways to show respect and give a meaningful gift of love to his

143

or her mate. . . . Doing only what is mutually agreeable sexually means that each partner will make sacrifices for the sake of intimacy."[4] Some specifics the McBurneys list that fit this criteria are oral sex, rear-entry vaginal penetration, initiation of sexual activity, positions for intercourse, and mutual masturbation.

Pleasurability. It must cause no pain physically, emotionally, or spiritually. If an activity you're engaged in isn't enjoyable, say the McBurneys, it will eventually cause resentment and distance between you. If it's a condition such as vaginitis or dryness, you can find treatment for that by seeking medical attention or applying a lubricant (K-Y Jelly, Astroglide, or Wet). Specifics outside of medical conditions would include sadomasochistic sex or bondage/domination fantasies and pornography. Typically when you get involved in these types of activities, they're considered tolerance stimulators. In other words, your tolerance becomes lower and you need increasing levels of the stimulation for the same sense of satisfaction.

Part of pleasurability also includes relationality. This is where pornography really becomes a problem. And I'm including romance novels and chat room sex talk in this category. In "Christian Sex Rules," the McBurneys address this problem:

> The relationship with a marriage partner may be replaced with various stimuli that are essentially fantasy based. . . . These disorders displace the relational dimension of sexuality. . . . The use of pornographic films from whatever source introduces this possible danger into your sexuality. Explicit sexual materials can provide sexual excitement and arousal, but that form of stimulation may erode your enjoyment of each other. Those images may also create a basic sense of dissatisfaction with yourself since most couples don't maintain or ever achieve the sensual appearance of porn actors and models. The whole industry is based on illusions and those lies can lead to death of your relationship as well as your sexual satisfaction.[5]

Perpetuating Genital Union. Whatever activity you and your spouse choose to engage in, it shouldn't substitute entirely for genital union. We were created for each other's bodies. There's a reason the penis fits into the vagina. Not only does it provide maximum pleasure, it molds us together as one. Specifics here include sexual aids (toys) and mutual masturbation.

When the Fairy-Tale Story Turns into Fantasyland

On Meghan's wedding night, she went into the restroom to prepare for the evening. She slipped into her sexy new negligee, sprayed on perfume, and fixed her makeup and hair. She wanted her wedding night to be perfect, a scene in which she would step out of the bathroom and her husband would grab her in his strong arms, passionately kiss her, and tell her how beautiful she was.

With one last glance in the mirror, she ran her hands down her body and slipped out into the bedroom where her lover was waiting. And watching ESPN.

No swooping up into his arms. No breathless, passionate remarks about her stunning beauty. No acknowledgment of her presence. That is, until she angrily stepped in front of the television.

Her husband tilted his head and said, "Let me just see the rest of this inning." Meghan responded with, "How about if you just watch the rest of the game?" and stormed back into the bathroom. He looked toward her and said, "What?" Poor clueless boy.

Fortunately, they are still married. But her advice? "Make sure you tell your fiancé before the wedding night that watching sports is off-limits. When I communicated clearly what I expected and he didn't have to read my mind, he did his best to follow through."

When Sex Hurts

Sex should not invariably cause pain. And any discomfort you may feel—especially if you are a virgin—can be overcome. If you discover intercourse to be painful, here are some possible reasons and what to do about them.

1. You may not be lubricated enough. Guys typically don't take a lot of foreplay. They're visually stimulated and they're ready to go. Gals need long, slow foreplay to ensure they're lubricated enough. You may want to pack a lubricant to take with you on your honeymoon. If you're concerned about buying some because of what the cashier or even your husband may think, choose to push those thoughts aside. Remember, this is about you enjoying the gift of sex.

2. You may have a psychological hang-up. In *Marriage Partnership*'s Real Sex column, columnists Dr. Louis and Melissa McBurney write, "Experiencing pain . . . creates anxiety about the possibility of having pain again. That fear becomes a barrier to arousal."[6] Allow yourself to relax. This isn't a competition. There's no time limit. Let your mind concentrate on the pleasure. Now is the time to explore each other. Caress, stroke, touch. Slowly. Try a different position: Place yourself on top of your husband. If the pain persists, talk about it with your spouse and decide for the time being not to concentrate on reaching orgasm, but rather focus on pleasuring each other.

The McBurneys suggest doing this by forgetting about intercourse and focusing on having fun:

> Take turns bringing the pleasure of physical touch to your mate. Begin with such things as back rubs, foot massage, and scalp or neck stimulation. Anything your mate enjoys except genital touch. Finding ways to bring enjoyment will allow bonding and displace fear. When these actions become natural and positive, begin to move toward some erotic stimulation. At first this might be kissing around the head and neck and going south from there. Breast stimulation, thighs, buttocks, and finally

genital massage can begin. Allow these to develop only as far as they feel good. Don't rush or force each other.

Ultimately the pleasuring should go to orgasm, but still taking turns and still avoiding intercourse. When you can achieve climax in this way, you may move toward mutuality, both of you pleasuring and receiving pleasure. Don't worry about genital union until it's a natural and desired culmination of your play.[7]

3. You may have a tight hymen or vagina or a medical condition. If you're properly lubricated and relaxed yet still feel persistent pain, you may want to consult your gynecologist to check for any physical problems.

Here's something you definitely do *not* want to do, however. You don't want to say or in other ways convey to your husband, "Let's just get this over with." That will wreak havoc not just in your physical relationship, but in all areas.

If sex doesn't feel good, be truthful with your husband. Let him know you want to enjoy sex with him, but your body doesn't want to cooperate. Then work together to find a solution. The best thing you can do is to talk to your spouse about it.

— Quick Tips —

Truly, your husband isn't as concerned about your weight as you are. He's more interested in your breasts!

Amanda, married four years

It's okay to be sexy.

Eileen, married two years

Have fun, make noise, groan, and nibble. Use slang, name your body parts. You'll be amazed at how great lovemaking will be.

Madelyn, married two years

If you are not a virgin and have already had sex with your fiancé, take a moment to recognize that your wedding night is different. The first time you have sex with your husband is sacred.

> Martha, married three years

If you don't have an orgasm the first night, that's okay. You may not get the hang of sex for a while. It took me a year! Instead of concentrating on what you aren't having, focus on enjoying the process and the stimulation.

> Carrie, married one year

Try reading the biblical book Song of Songs out loud to your sweetie. Talk about a turn-on — right from the pages of the Bible.

> Eileen, married two years

If you have problems adjusting to sex after a period of time, you may want to consider seeing a Christian counselor. Most are trained to instruct couples in sex therapy.

> Eileen, married two years

— Quick Quips —

"Whoa! *This* is flesh of my flesh and bone of my bones." — Adam, the first groom, viewing his bride, Eve, for the first time.

> Genesis 2:23; the John Ortberg translation

Unleashing a childlike curiosity, becoming delightfully uninhibited, trying new things,

and being playmates are all part of this vital
component of exciting intercourse. . . . Some
practice and experimenting can create great
variety and immense romantic pleasure.

Dr. Douglas Rosenau

THIRTEEN

The Honeymoon Hiatus

Extending the Wedding

Scott and I had many out-of-town guests attend our wedding, and we realized we wouldn't be able to spend much time with them on our wedding day. They had made a special effort to come to the ceremony, and we wanted to thank them by spending extra time with them. So several weeks before the wedding, we decided to extend the festivities to include a postnuptial get-together. We contacted a local hotel—the same one we'd recommended to our guests—and booked a conference room and continental breakfast. It would be an informal time. No decorations, little cleanup, lots of talk time.

My only concern with having a "continuation reception" the day after the wedding was my fear that people would joke about Scott and me having wedding night sex. But I was pleased that no one cracked any jokes or made any tacky remarks. Everyone was gracious, and the event was a success. We spent the entire morning chatting, laughing, and bonding. The best part was when we went to pay our bill, the manager said, "What breakfast and room?" I thought he'd lost his mind. "If you leave that room the way you found it," he continued, "I won't know you used it, and I won't charge you. Consider it a wedding present from us." That was a several-hundred-dollar present!

Another bride, Jeane, and her husband, Tyson, did something similar. They gathered with their closest friends at a convenience store/fast-food place the morning after the wedding, sat, relaxed, and talked. "The best part is that you're not worried about the wedding," says Jeane. "You can just relax and enjoy your friends and family."

Starting the Honeymoon

Obviously, while everyone has her preferences about how to start the honeymoon, I'd suggest something Scott and I fell blindly into: Don't rush to get to your destination. In other words, if you get married on Saturday night and your reception isn't over until midnight, don't rush to the airport for a 7:00 A.M. flight. You really need to rest. Why not book your flight for a little later, say in the afternoon? That way, you can sleep in and come down somewhat from the wedding festivities, and you can enjoy the *process* of going on your honeymoon. While Scott and I had planned to leave at noon for our trip, we ended up not leaving until closer to 3:00 P.M. After the postwedding breakfast, we went back to my parents' house to collect some things and stuck around to talk about the wedding. My parents and others were eager to share their excitement about how beautiful it was. It was a great debriefing for us. And it was good to hear the neat things that had happened that Scott and I didn't know about. Yes, those people could share those tidbits after your honeymoon, but they might forget certain details. Why not hear them while they're fresh? So we went to lunch, talked, unwound, *then* left for our honeymoon. While that's not what we had originally planned, I'm glad it ended that way. It left me with wonderful memories. And how cool to hear people give you details of how beautiful you looked. Soak it up!

Where to Go?

Whenever I fantasized about my honeymoon—the exotic locale, the sunsets, the long walks, the romance—I imagined my new spouse and me wandering through the streets of a European country, Italy or Scotland or Ireland. Or we'd enjoy the sun, warmth, and beaches of the Bahamas.

I can say honestly, however, that when I considered my honeymoon, Florida never once crossed my mind as a destination—and especially not traveling through the state by motorcycle.

Thus I learned an important lesson in unmet expectations for marriage: Sometimes you make sacrifices because you love your husband. Scott planned our honeymoon, and since we had less than three months to prepare, we decided to go easy, then take the exotic trip for our first-year anniversary. That's when I thought, *Aruba for the honeymoon, Italy for our anniversary. That works.* However, there seemed to be some miscommunication between my betrothed and me. "Taking it easy" to him meant motorcycling through the Florida Keys and the Everglades.

Somehow looking at alligators just didn't seem all that romantic. I kept thinking he was kidding. He wasn't.

The one good reason I didn't throw a royal tantrum was because I was already flustered over planning a wedding that would take place two states away in less than three months.

So for our honeymoon we rented a truck, put the motorcycle on the truck bed, and drove from Ohio to Florida, where we unloaded the bike at a Wendy's parking lot in Daytona Beach, parked the truck at the Daytona Beach airport, and drove south.

We'd planned that first day on the bike to be our longest ride. Our goal was to drive five hours to Miami, where we'd spend the night before heading to the Keys. That sounded good in theory. Yet we neglected to take into account Miami rush-hour traffic. And Scott made no hotel reservations anywhere. That's not normally a problem—except the Winston Cup NASCAR races were in Homestead, the town situated between Miami, the Keys, and the Everglades—all the places we were visiting for our honeymoon. That meant we had to go by there in order to get to our destination. Imagine spending hours driving all over the southern part of Florida just to find one hotel room. We finally did—in a questionable part of Miami where we got the penthouse for $70. The guests looked like stereotypical drug dealers you see on television (the chains and rolls of cash didn't help). The pillows didn't have chocolates on them—they had a note about how to keep safe from intruders. That was when I stepped into the bathroom and had a nice little cry, after which I pulled myself together and realized where we stayed might not live up to my expectations, but I was spending time with my husband and we were making memories. I just hoped we'd live long enough to reminisce.

We figured driving to Key West, more than a hundred miles from the mainland, would guarantee we'd be able to find a hotel room away from the NASCAR races. Well, that was true. However, we discovered Key West was hosting the International Speed Boat races, and all the hotel rooms were booked or tripled in price.

There's an old saying, "Expect the unexpected." That should be your motto for your honeymoon.

? Did You Know?

According to *The Don't Sweat Guide for Weddings,* several cultures used to have the custom of spending your honeymoon at your mother-in-law's house.[1] Talk about some unmet expectations!

Surprised by Exhaustion

The biggest "unexpected" will be exhaustion. Your honeymoon should be relaxing, fun, wonderful, exciting, and romantic. Actually, it could be all of those things if you took your honeymoon about six months after your wedding.

One newlywed, Corrie, summed it up best: "All I wanted to do was sleep!" Another bride, Amy, agreed, "I was surprised at how tired I was during the honeymoon. I thought we'd have all this energy and we'd get to go play on our first vacation together. But I was exhausted! We just slept a lot and spent most of our time resting because we had just spent a year planning for our wedding."

Stress Relievers

If you find yourself exhausted or let down, allow yourself not to have to do, do, do. Take this time to really relax and enjoy your spouse. You are now a Missus!

Why not plan a low-key honeymoon where you can have privacy and be able to rest? I know some couples who traveled through Europe. While that sounds wonderful, you may be too fatigued and stressed from planning the ceremony of the century to really appreciate the sights. Plus you can add jet lag and road-weariness into the mix.

Jeane and her husband decided to honeymoon in a nearby town at a resort/bed & breakfast. They were able to go there after the reception and stay for the duration of their honeymoon. "I wanted to go someplace close so we could focus on relaxing rather than traveling," says Jeane. She asked a friend to precheck them in earlier on their wedding day and to get the room ready for them with chocolates, candles, and goodies for their time together.

"The great thing," says Jeane, "is that we were able to go back to the same room for Valentine's Day, our anniversary, and other special days. We made it a tradition."

The honeymoon is the beginning of your life together—it's not the goal of your life together. As a matter of fact, many women place such a high expectation on this time that if it doesn't measure up, if they don't enjoy each and every moment of their time on the honeymoon, they think something's wrong with them. The honeymoon can be great, but it won't be—and shouldn't be!—the high point of your married life. (I can say this with confidence considering I rode on the back of a motorcycle for ten days.) Yes, it can be a time of great memory making. But it's not all downhill from there.

One bride found this to be true. She and her husband spent a tense honeymoon in the Bahamas. "I was so tired and wanted to have everything just right, that when it wasn't I took it out on my husband," she says. "Now I see how immature and hurtful I was, but at the time it was all about reaching the ideal."

Another bride, Amy, also found this to be true. She enjoyed her honeymoon but was so exhausted, it wasn't the picture of perfection she had imagined. However, about four months into their marriage, she and her husband, Trei, attended a wedding in Hawaii. "I enjoyed that trip much more than my honeymoon," says Amy. "We were relaxed and rested. We didn't have any 'performance' anxiety, and we were familiar with each other by that point. That helped us to have a great time. I almost wish we would have taken a shorter honeymoon, then taken an extended honeymoon several months later."

Glitches and Mishaps

You may drink the water in some foreign country and end up with diarrhea or suffer from motion sickness and spend your days vomiting over the side of the cruise ship. You may start

155

your menstrual cycle, catch a cold, or be sunburned—even though you didn't plan for that.

What do you do when you experience the glitches of everyday life? Keep your sense of humor! Try to find something, *anything,* funny. If nothing else, your experience will make a great story. Cheryl and her husband, Aaron, can attest to that. They were on the ideal honeymoon: a trip to Tahiti. They had a hut that sat on the ocean and had a ladder that went down into the water. The first day they arrived, they decided to take a swim. Since the water was choppy, they clung tightly to the ladder as they descended into the water. The ladder had a type of algae growing on it that made it a little slippery, but nothing that made them concerned—until the next day when Cheryl awoke to discover her entire body covered with an itchy poison ivy type rash. Then Aaron also contracted it. They called for the island physician, who fortunately made house calls and gave them some calamine-like ointment. Unfortunately though, the ointment didn't help. Cheryl and Aaron spent their dream honeymoon stuck in their hut playing cards. They couldn't touch each other for the entire honeymoon. "It wasn't funny at the time," Cheryl admits, "but we can laugh about it now."

Another couple, Amy and Todd, had planned an exciting trip to London for their honeymoon. She was thrilled to visit a place she had never been, and since Todd had been there before, she knew they would visit some of the little-known tourist spots. She never anticipated, however, that they would spend their first day in London walking the London canal system—a complex system that winds its way over miles of London. "I was out of shape and had blisters all over my feet," Amy says. But that wasn't the worst part: "He wanted to walk it again the next day! It didn't seem to matter to him that I was walking on blisters. That's when I started to cry and thought, *I want to go home! I've married the wrong man.*"

Your honeymoon is a time to create fun memories, or in the case of mishaps, funny memories. Regardless of what happens, you can make or break your honeymoon. Choose to acknowledge that the situation stinks but you're going to make the best of it. When I stood in the bathroom of that stereotypical, drug dealer infested Miami hotel and felt sorry for myself, I felt God speak to me deep within my soul. He said, *Ginger, your husband wants to have a wonderful honeymoon too — and you have the power to ruin this for him.* That helped me put things in perspective. "If I survive this night, God," I prayed, "then I'll have the best honeymoon anybody has ever had." Well, we survived, and while it wasn't the *best* honeymoon, if I could do it over, I'd still choose to go on a motorcycle trip to Florida.

Sleeping Adjustments

My friend Karen says marriage is like having a slumber party with your best friend every night. That's a great idea, except at some point you'll actually want to slumber. Some studies indicate that almost 30 percent of marriages are affected by sleeping disorders.

Welcome to married life, which includes the joys of discovering your husband's annoying sleep habits — and having him discover yours! If you like to take your half out of the middle, or if he has sleep apnea and quits breathing while he sleeps or snores so loudly the people in the next room start pounding on your wall, you are in store for marital adjustments.

Or maybe your husband just has certain quirky bedtime rituals. Maybe he has to sleep on the side closest to the door. One bride was surprised that her husband has to have the window open and a fan blowing — regardless of the season. "I spent the entire honeymoon sleeping under a pile of blankets!" she says.

Plus you are still getting accustomed to sleeping with someone in the same bed. This one took me quite a while because I felt as if I kept rolling into the center of the bed.

If you have trouble sleeping, try a pair of earplugs or explain that you have difficulty getting to sleep and try to fall asleep before your husband. If that still doesn't work, researchers suggest you ask your spouse not to eat food or drink alcohol within three hours of going to bed and make sure he sleeps on his side. If you still have no success, once you return from the honeymoon, you may want to contact a physician for other options.

— Quick Tips —

The best thing I took on my honeymoon was an air freshener and candles for when my husband used the bathroom. You'll be amazed at how much happier you'll be.

Jeane, married four years

If you choose to go to a resort, make sure it's an all-inclusive package so you don't have to worry about money or keeping to a budget.

Amy, married four years

Don't forget to take sunscreen. I got burned on my honeymoon, which definitely put a damper on our time together. Forget sex; I could barely stand putting on a bra.

Madelyn, married two years

Once you've left for your honeymoon, take a few moments to contact your parents and new in-laws to let them know you've arrived safely at your destination and to thank them for the wedding day and for how much you appreciate their helpfulness.

Jennifer, married three months

FOURTEEN

What Do You Mean the Honeymoon's Over?

I t was the last day of our honeymoon, and Scott and I were on our way back to my parents' house to pick up our wedding gifts. As we came upon the exit for my parents' hometown, I felt this overwhelming sense of sadness wash over me. In just a few short hours, our honeymoon would be a memory.

I looked at Scott and said, "We're schmucks again."

"Excuse me?"

I sighed. "For the past four months we've been special. I've been engaged, and everyone has oohed and aahed over my ring and wanted to hear every detail about the proposal and our gift registry and the wedding plans. Then on our wedding day, I was the center of everyone's attention. I looked beautiful and was dressed in the most expensive gown I'll probably ever wear. We were congratulated and toasted. After the wedding, we told everyone we were on our honeymoon, and again, everyone gave us the star treatment. Now we're just a married couple. We have nothing special we're planning for. No one's going to 'ooh' and 'aah' over us. We're schmucks again."

"Oh."

All good things must come to an end—which in most honeymoon cases will be in about seven days. At the end of that time, it's back to life as usual. Now what?

Wedding Withdrawal

Once I returned from the honeymoon, it felt as if all of a sudden I went from frenzy to dead calm. I actually focused on my duties at my job rather than lunging for the phone every time it rang, thinking it was the florist or the caterer calling. It was a bittersweet passage moving from the land of "nearly-wed" to "newlywed."

After one of my coworkers returned from her honeymoon, she made the comment, "It feels as though my life now lacks purpose. My entire life was spent trying to find a man and get married. Well, I've done that, so now what do I have left to look forward to?"

Sure, you almost had a nervous breakdown and seriously considered visiting a psychotherapist while you were planning the wedding. Absolutely, you went through several bottles of aspirin. But now that it's over, you kind of miss it. You may feel let down after the wedding. Some people even call it post-wedding depression.

The worst part is that no one asks to see your ring or asks about the wedding or honeymoon plans. The FedEx man no longer brings packages to your door. And really, not everyone wants to see your wedding photos. And they especially don't want a framed copy of your wedding photo for Christmas. You just can't seem to understand what the rest of the world's problem is. *Don't they realize I am a newlywed?* you think. *I just made the biggest commitment of my life to the greatest man in the world! Someone should still be interested.*

The hard truth is that pretty much other than your mom and your husband, no one else is interested anymore. They're thinking, *Let it go; get on with your life. Please.*

Callie experienced just such a letdown after the wedding planning: "I had so much fun organizing the event that afterward I felt really sad. What helped was that I knew some friends who were getting married, so I was a wealth of knowledge and could get involved by volunteering to help my friends. I was thrilled to give referrals, help with invitations, scope out the best deals, and help any way I could."

Another way to move your focus toward the future is to set goals for trips or events you can plan now that you're married. Set your sights on setting up your household. Paint a room. Plan a holiday get-together for friends or family. Or plan periodic long-weekend getaways. If money is tight, check for online or off-season deals. By planning those types of festivities, you can transition more easily to the future and the excitement that lies ahead for you and your husband. It doesn't have to be anything big, expensive, or fancy. But the anticipation of planning and setting a goal is a great motivator to help you move in the right direction.

Unusual and Wacky Wedding Gifts

I was so naïve when I got married. I thought most people would give us gifts that were elegant. Or at least presents from the bridal registry I had spent many endless hours poring over and defending to Scott. ("Of course we need the crystal salad spinner/egg chopper/cheese slicer. Duh.") And most people did just that. To be fair, you'll get some wonderful, creative presents. I think of the album filled with photos from a bridal shower, our rehearsal, and wedding one of my bridesmaids gave me. Or the "trousseau" of lingerie my matron of honor "bestowed" upon me.

But, ah, there were also the doozies. The old—not to be confused with antique—angel wrapped in kleenex and placed in a used and scotch-taped box comes to mind. And of course, let's remember those friends and family members who not only bypassed the bridal registry list—they bypassed the gift. For instance, several weeks ago I was talking about this book to a friend of mine, Jennifer, who's been married nineteen years. I joked with her and told her I wasn't going to interview her since she's been married so long she probably doesn't remember all the nitty-gritty details about her wedding. She said, "You know what, Ginger? I can tell you that I am still waiting on a gift from my aunt who made a big deal about wanting to be invited to the wedding." Touché.

Take a look at some of the other weird wedding gifts brides received:

A $5 plastic stool/TV remote holder

Stained purple towels

A bottle of wine dressed up in cowboy hat and chaps

A box of Jordan almonds (Don't most brides give these to the *guests* as reception favors?)

A 1970s burnt orange/brown enamel stockpot. At least it had the lid.

Canary yellow towels—none of which were on the registry. $5

Also, you can plan on receiving several of one item. Leann registered for six towels and received eight. Scott and I registered for one mini food processor and ended up with four. Some people won't even bother with the registration. Lori received a lovely glass jar of pistachios. She never registered for them, but her coworkers enjoyed the contents. These are the times when gratitude is important — but equally important is the gift receipt.

Thank-You Cards

Two weeks after our wedding, I received a phone call at work that went something like this:

"Ginger?"

"Yes?"

"I've been a little worried that you didn't receive the single serving of silverware I sent."

"I did receive it. Thank you so much for sending it. That was so thoughtful of you."

Silence, then:

"Yes, well, I was just concerned because you know I haven't received my thank-you card."

"Oh, you're right. You know Scott and I just got back from our honeymoon, so I haven't had a chance to start writing those."

Technically, according to the etiquette books I've read, you are allowed one to three months to complete your thank-you cards — and I used every last day. (I also wanted to photocopy a paragraph that discussed the three-month deadline and subtly include it in with the thank-you cards, but I wasn't too sure how subtle it would be.)

One idea that helps avoid those concerned calls is to send gift acknowledgment cards. Then you can write your thank-yous when you are more settled. It can be as simple as a postcard that says, "We received your present." Although you may want to word it more elegantly.

One other note about writing thank-yous: Now that I'm married, I can see clearly that there are role definitions for a husband and wife. There are some things men simply are not wired to do. Writing thank-you notes is one of them. My friend Jeane agrees: "My husband wasn't helpful with the thank-you cards. Men aren't. That's just reality. I'm sorry if you think differently."

Beware if you have your husband write out the thank-you cards. You may want to have him write them only to his own family and friends because, according to Dan Zevin, author of *The Nearly-Wed Handbook*, they'll read something like this: "Dear Mrs. Schnitzer, thanks for the, um, thing. Your friend, Stan."[1]

Stop the Madness!

You'd think the stress would end after the wedding. Oh no, my friend. Now comes the fun part of adjusting to living with someone else. It probably includes moving into a new space and unpacking all of your belongings—boxes and boxes of items you haven't used or seen in decades. And if you're an "older" bride, that means you will have two already established households to combine. This was a huge stressor to me—so much so that it just about paralyzed me. I felt so overwhelmed when I moved all my things into my husband's *really* small house. Somehow we had to make room for an entire household (mine) in an already established household (his), plus add in all the wedding presents (ours). Literally the boxes went to the ceiling. I would look around the mess of boxes and piles and cry. "How am I supposed to unpack all my stuff?" I'd ask Scott. "I mean, I can unpack it, but then where do I put it?" I felt as though I were an intruder: It wasn't *my* house, and these weren't really *my* things. This was Scott's house I was invading.

Scott is the master organizer, and he and I decided to take baby steps. I'd try to unpack one box every other evening after work, and Scott and I would jostle things around until we could find a place for the contents. He also hung extra shelves, and we purchased some bookcases. The transition took most of our first year because we went slowly, but eventually I began to feel like less of an intruder and more like I belonged in our home.

Finding Your Identity

Another difficult adjustment for me was trying to figure out my new role. I'd always been a single woman known as Ginger McFarland. I had established my own identity, my own career, my own person, my own fiercely independent nature. That was who I was. And I *liked* who I was. Now I was going to be someone different. And I wasn't really sure who that someone was. There were moments when I even felt as if I were betraying myself or abandoning my family.

Amy had similar thoughts: "I remember as Trei and I were driving away from the reception, I thought, *Who am I now? Who is Amy Tatum?* I had always been Amy Robinson. I had this whole life in this community where everyone knew me as Amy Robinson, and now I was somebody different. I was somebody I didn't know. And I was a wreck. I became so emotional. I thought, *This is my life now? I'm driving away with this guy? This is ridiculous.*" The worst part was that after the honeymoon they were moving to a different state for Trei's job. "It was so hard because I was going someplace where I'd be known as Amy Tatum. Nobody cared who Amy Robinson was. That was difficult for me to let go of," Amy says.

The Bible tells us that the two of you will become one — two people joined together as one unit. The problem I encountered was whose one do we become? A friend of mine and I discussed this before her wedding. "I love my fiancé," she said. "But what happens if I lose who I am? I like me." Her fears are well founded. After all, it's the bride who changes her name, who goes from being an independent gal to "wife" then possibly "mom" — for the rest of her life.

You may be surprised by an overwhelming sadness or grief when you begin your new life. One bride experienced a deep sense of loneliness when, after the reception, she returned to the church to collect her things. She went to the ladies' room to remove her wedding dress, and no one was there to assist her.

"I just broke down," she says. "I felt so alone, and no one was there to help me. I felt like I was leaving everything I knew."

The contradiction of weddings is that you're starting, or giving birth to, a new life. Yet at the same time, you are leaving behind, or burying, your old life. You are entering new territory and leaving familiar ground. It's only natural to experience sadness, loneliness, or fear. The best help you can give yourself is to acknowledge what you are feeling and allow for some time to grieve. It's okay to cry over the loss. And it's okay to share those feelings with your husband. While he may not understand, he needs you to be honest about your thoughts and fears. When you deal with them head-on, you will be able to move forward and regain the joy of your newly married status.

It can become overwhelming because you have to decide who you want to be. The wedding is fun, but then you discover, "Oh, I have a marriage now." Getting married means you have a new identity, that of wife. I remember how much I struggled with deciding if I'd keep my maiden name or change it. Do you know in other cultures you keep your maiden name? Take for instance Mexico, where you take both your mother's and father's surnames. Then when you get married you drop your mother's, but keep your father's. I liked being a McFarland. Now I was going to be somebody else, with somebody else's last name and a whole new set of traditions and ways of doing things.

It's normal to ask, *Who am I?*

I made a comment to my grandmother one day about the difficulty I was having with making a name change. I expected her to make some statement that would brush off my concerns. After all, she and my grandfather have been married sixty years. She's used to the name change. And back when she got married, that wasn't even an issue; you just did it. But she looked at me and confessed, "I understand, Ginger. Do you know when your grandpa and I had been married thirty years, I was in a store writing a check and I signed my maiden name. I hadn't thought about that for years, but it had been in my subconscious that whole time."

Part of the problem with a name change is what do you change it to? Do you keep your maiden name? Take your husband's name? Hyphenate your maiden and married names? Combine your maiden name and your married surname? (I had a teacher in first grade who did that: Ms. Hausfeld. I was always confused about what her husband's name was.)

Changes Checklist

If you opt to change your name—whether taking your spouse's or hyphenating, you need to do a few things after the honeymoon to make it official. You'll want to do this sooner rather than later. I have a friend, Anna, who after being married five years, has yet to change her social security information. Keep in mind many of these paperwork changes are going to require that you have a notarized copy of your marriage license. A Kinko's copy won't do. Make sure to update the following:

Driver's license. You can do this at any DMV office—but you may want to go on any day but Saturday, or you'll wait in line.

All your insurance policies: automobile, motorcycle, life, health, homeowner's

Social Security records. Contact your nearest Social Security office or go online at www.ssa.gov and request a form to make the change.

Stocks or financial portfolio

Bank accounts. You'll also need to decide how you're going to combine your finances. (We'll discuss this later. See p. 177)

Credit cards

Voter registration

Apartment leases or home mortgage and utility records

Employment records

Anyone you deal with professionally in your business. Send a brief letter letting them know you've just gotten married and what your new name is. That also helps them see how your new name will be spelled. This isn't usually an issue if you're marrying a man whose last name is Smith or Jones. But marry a man whose last name is Saengdarapheth or Rivadeneira or Kolbaba and your business associates will greatly appreciate your thoughtfulness. You may even want to spell your name phonetically to help them pronounce it.

The sooner you handle these issues, the less stress you'll have. Plus it will give you time later to write those thank-you cards.

Other people's names change too after the wedding — or at least what you call them may change. This can be as confusing as keeping track of your own name change. "I had an issue with what to call my husband's parents after the wedding," says Madelyn, married two years. "I'm uncomfortable calling them Mom and Dad because it feels as if I'm being disloyal to my own parents. To be honest, I try not to call them anything. I just talk to them. I can't call them by their first names — and I certainly can't call them 'Mr. and Mrs. Slattery.'"

Families have different preferences when it comes to names. The level of formality between adults and children, for example, can vary. Eileen, married two years, found this out when she spent time with her husband's extended family. "My husband was reared to call his aunts and uncles with the prefaces 'Aunt' and 'Uncle.' In my family, I always addressed them by their first names only," she says. "To this day, I have difficulty calling his aunt 'Aunt Linda' when I don't even do that for my own family!"

The other part of the problem is trying to let go of being independent. Scott and I hobbled along as I struggled to allow myself to be interdependent. I felt as if I needed to be financially responsible for the family. I had to be the one who was accountable.

Jeane had her identity crisis when she and her husband, Tyson, went to the bank to combine their bank accounts. "I thought, *Wait a minute, this is* my *money,"* says Jeane. "That really bothered me because I wasn't sure what to do."

Beth had trouble on this end too. She got married when she was forty something. She had always been financially independent and was used to taking care of herself. "It was difficult for me to make this transformation in which I was allowing someone else to take care of me," Beth admits. "My husband, Dean, would say, 'Beth, you're going into your single mode again.'"

What adds to the difficulty is that our culture tells us women have to do it all ourselves—even when we're married. But if we fall into that lie, we do damage to our marriages. Just look at the divorce rate and tell me I'm wrong.

Scott still has to remind me at times that I don't have to carry the burden of life by myself. He's there to help and that has been a comfort. But it takes a lot of trust and time. The other comfort is in knowing that I'm not really losing who I used to be. I'm taking that with me and using it to build my marriage on my strengths from my single years.

Leaving and Cleaving

This is yet another adjustment in which you switch allegiances. From your wedding day on, you will need to consider the desires and needs of your spouse above all others.

Depending on how close-knit your family is, this realization may bring some sadness with it. You may entertain such thoughts as, *I'm leaving my family! I'm not going to be part of that family anymore.* Lisa experienced this. "I kept thinking about how we wouldn't go on family vacations anymore," she says. "It won't just be us. And holidays will be different."

You are leaving behind your family to establish a new family. In essence you are moving beyond your past. In his book *Covenant Marriage,* Dr. Fred Lowery tells of a wedding custom on the Indonesian island of Java that illustrates this concept.

On the day before her wedding, the bride calls together all of her friends. In their presence she burns the things associated with her past life, including dolls, toys, and other cherished items of her childhood. At that point her friends console her over the loss of these past treasures by giving her presents — things identified with maturity and representing her new life. Marriage is the time to leave behind childish things, childish behavior, and childlike attitudes, as well as childlike dependency on parents.[2]

Only when we recognize that the past is part of us but no longer holds us, can we move confidently into the future.

The Protective Bubble Myth

On their wedding day, few brides think about the upcoming hurdles they'll face in marriage. Yes, we say we'll love and honor each other in sickness and in health, through good times and bad. But really, who dwells on the "in sickness" or "through bad times" part? Yet Jesus tells us, "On earth you will have many trials and sorrows" (John 16:33). He could have easily inserted "in marriage you will have many trials and sorrows." Because you will. Many of us enter marriage with this expectation that love will protect us from hardship, that we have this unburstable protective bubble surrounding us. Madelyn discovered there was no such bubble when she married her husband, who had a difficult ex-wife. "She would just walk into our house — even after we told her she couldn't. She would make 'innocent' cutting remarks or comments about my husband. She was cunning and manipulative and tried to come between my husband and me."

Stacey discovered her husband looked at pornography. Beth discovered her husband was in financial debt, to the point that the court threatened to throw him in jail. My husband and I built a house and were sued for a personal injury that threatened

170

to take our house and all our assets. Krista's military husband was sent overseas to the Middle East.

Automobile accidents, dark family secrets, diseases, financial troubles, sexual inadequacies, the list goes on. Jesus was right: "On earth you will have many trials and sorrows." That's a guarantee. Bella and her husband became involved in a huge argument on their honeymoon, and her husband threatened her with divorce and began a pattern of emotional and verbal abuse that almost broke Bella's spirit until she got help.

Yet there's another part of that guarantee. Jesus says, "But take heart! I have overcome the world" (John 16:33, NIV).

How you deal with those trials and sorrows will determine the success of your marriage. We can lean into the brokenness and selfishness that would come easily. Or we can stand firm, pray consistently, accept the rough road, choose joy over sorrow, decide to trust that God, who is our refuge and place of safety (Ps. 91:2), will work to cause all things to turn out for the good. He will fight for you (Exod. 14:14). Determine to fight for the marriage rather than against it. Keep focused on God and on each other. Those choices may not take away the rough road, but they will make it much easier to deal with.

— Quick Tips —

Be creative with your thank-you cards! We used one of our wedding photos and had it made into thank-you cards so they would be more of a keepsake than just something your guest would get and throw away. And we discovered several of our guests framed them!

Kay, married three years

Make sure you duplicate the gift list for each set of parents. They love to see the gifts their friends and family give.[3]

Ann Platz and Susan Wales

171

Be prepared for your income taxes to increase
once you get married.

Eileen, married two years

— Quick Quips —

It is more blessed to give than to receive — for
example, wedding presents.

H. L. Mencken

A word to new brides: If you want to be
remembered forever, don't write a thank-you note
for a wedding gift.

Edward L. Rankin, Jr.

The whole name change issue is huge! Not just
the last name, but also the middle name. Do you
use your given middle name or do you switch and
use your maiden name as your middle name and
drop your given middle name? Or do you keep
them all, which makes for a lot of initials or a long
name on your banking checks? Yet another thing
to deliberate over!

Karen, married one year

FIFTEEN

Keep the Joy Alive— You're Married!

You are now set to begin the most wonderful part of life—living with your best friend. But no matter how close you are, there will undoubtedly be some friction as you settle into married life. Part of the adjustment period is adapting to particulars your husband is used to but that you are not. Jeane found this in regard to breakfast. "I never made breakfast—I didn't even eat breakfast!" Jeane confesses. "But my husband does, so I've learned to make a small sacrifice of waking a little earlier to make his meal. That took some getting used to." Making your bed is another one. Even setting up household chores can cause a shock to your system. "I never worked so hard in my life!" Jeane says. "I feel more responsible now. It's a bigger deal to me if I don't make my bed. When I was single, I didn't care." One thing that may help this adjustment period is to talk with your spouse about the expectations each of you has. Household tasks are a biggie — and can cause immense amounts of stress and frustration. If your husband came from a family in which his mother did everything, you either have to accept that you're stepping into Mom's shoes, or you have to explain to your husband that your style is different. Be careful not to make demands or threats. Take the onus upon yourself and explain, "One of the things that would make me feel loved and special is if you would help me with the dishes each night or take out the trash."

Here are some other adjustments you may not have considered:

Grocery shopping. You may be used to your grocery store; you know the layout where everything is located. Now you have to learn your way around a new grocery store. What used to be an in-and-out five-minute trip now takes you fifteen minutes, and that's just finding the aisle where the item is located.

Cooking. I was surprised that I now had to cook — or learn to cook. I was used to going home after work and preparing a salad, pasta, or cereal. Scott expected an actual meal: meat, vegetables, starch, drink. That was a huge adjustment for me. It still is, actually. Comedian Rita Rudner sums it up best: "I read recipes the same way I read science fiction: I get to the end and think, *Well, that's not going to happen.*"

Loss of privacy. When I was single I would come home, flip on the television or grab a book, and enjoy the evening quietly. Now I share the television. And I've done less reading than ever.

Friends. One bride says, "I noticed some of my single friends who were still getting together all of a sudden weren't including me. If I didn't call them, I wouldn't hear from them. I was no longer included in what they were doing. That was a hard adjustment."

Grieving Your Singleness

About two or three months into my matrimonial bliss, I felt sad. I wasn't necessarily depressed—or maybe I was. I just had this deep sense of sorrow that I couldn't explain or shake. *Why am I so miserable?* I'd wonder. I was happily married. I loved my husband. I loved being a Mrs. But I knew something just wasn't quite right. So one day when I was talking with my friend Amy, I mentioned it to her.

"I can't figure out why I'm feeling this way. I shouldn't be," I told her.

"Oh Ginger, you're experiencing what we all experience to some degree," she said wisely. "You're grieving your singleness."

So that was it! All of a sudden I felt a little lighter. I was mourning that which had past from my life. Leaving singleness for marriage is a major life-changing event. It's a death, in a sense.

I felt understood when Amy verbalized what I had been feeling.

"Did you experience this after you got married?"

She laughed. "I sure did. But I got through it, and so will you."

It's only natural to experience feelings of depression or sadness after—or even before—your wedding. You've put to death your past and need to say good-bye to it, to acknowledge that your life has moved into a new phase. Even if you hated every moment of your unmarried life, something will probably come up that will make you grieve the change a little.

For some women, the grieving comes out in a good, long torrent of tears. They cleanse their spirits, and then they're okay. For others it takes a little longer.

175

I thought I was doing okay until soon after I returned to work after the honeymoon. One brilliant co-worker called to inform me that I'd gone from being a GEM (my maiden initials) to a GEK (my married initials), which she pronounced *geek*. I thanked her for ingeniously pointing that out. Then I hung up the phone, shut the door to my office, and promptly began to weep.

Martha Williamson makes the wise observation, "When we agree to marry someone, the reality of what we are about to do has a way of presenting itself to us by degrees."[1]

Cry, mourn, and even eulogize your former life. Take some time to be alone to think about this life change. You don't have to be ashamed or feel guilty. This is a normal part of life. Change creates some sense of sadness. And when you've grieved that which you have lost, you will clear a path to engage fully in that which you have gained.

What's So Great about Being Married?

- Being able to say "My husband"
- Sex
- Writing "Mrs." before your name
- Waking beside your best friend
- Having a companion
- Being safely vulnerable with another person
- Growing more mature—even when it hurts
- Having someone hold you after you've had a nightmare
- Inside jokes
- Snuggling up to your husband in bed to keep warm

A United Front

Now that you're married, you don't have just one family of origin to consider—you have three: your family, your in-laws, and you and your husband, since as a couple you are now a family unit. And that's the family that takes precedence. If you begin to feel railroaded by family pressures, be honest and express your feelings. Set ground rules. First, talk to your husband: "I appreciate how helpful your mom is, but when she shows up unexpectedly at our house and stays, I feel pressured to drop my plans and what I'm doing to entertain her. Can we establish some boundaries as a couple and present them to our families?"

If and when you do confront the opposing party, make sure you and your spouse are a united front. You don't have to defend your position. State your feelings, show that you and your spouse have made this decision together, and don't fall into the dangerous trap of allowing a family member to play you against your mate.

Getting Advice

When you and your husband hit a brick wall where neither of you can agree, be careful about whom you go to for advice. You can go to your parents, but remember that they will be biased on your side, and his parents will probably be biased on his side. If that's the case, you're not doing your marriage any favors. You want to seek advice from wise people who won't take sides, who love both of you, and who are cheering for your marriage—not for you as an individual. Seek out someone who doesn't have a skewed view and who will speak the truth to you.

For Richer or Poorer

Hopefully, one of the topics you discussed before you got married was your finances. If not, now's the time. You'll want to come to an agreement about who will do the bookkeeping and pay the bills. Will you have a joint checking account or separate? I know one couple who have three accounts—a "yours, mine, and ours" approach to their finances. They each have a set amount they direct deposit into their joint account to cover living expenses, tithe, and monthly bills. Then they put a certain amount into investments such as retirement and savings. Lastly, they put a smaller amount into their personal accounts for separate discretionary spending (personal items, clothes, birthday presents).

However you choose to combine your finances, you'll want to sit down and talk with each other to make sure you're on the same page.

The "D" Word

Beth received a shock during her honeymoon. She and her husband got into a heated argument about "something trivial. I don't even remember what it was," she says. In the heat of the argument, her husband threw out the word *divorce*.

"I never felt so insecure in my life," she says. "It has really affected my marriage and my self-esteem." All of a sudden, what was supposed to be a safe and vulnerable place became compromised. Instead of resting assured in her spouse's commitment, she questioned it.

Make a promise to your spouse that you will never, *ever* utter the word *divorce* when talking about your relationship. Not in anger, not in despair, not *ever*. Make a pact that divorce will not be an option. If you leave it as an "out," in case things get too tough or things don't work out or you're not happy, you'll never be able to truly experience the complete and vulnerable joy of being yourself or of commitment. Consider marriage a lifetime experience.

Remarriage

With the prevalence of divorce in our society, there's a chance you may have married someone who's been married before. Lori

Graham Bakker, in her book *More Than I Could Ever Ask,* discusses what marrying a man who's been married before requires: "In every divorce and remarriage where children are involved, the new wife has to come to terms with the existence of the former wife and her continued presence in the restructured family unit. It's seldom an easy adjustment."[2] For her, that would be an understatement: Her husband's ex is the larger-than-life Tammy Faye.

Let's face it, if this is your situation, ex-wives are an unfortunate part of your hubby's past. But they *are* a part. And there are some, though not all, who want to make sure you *know* they were part of his intimate history. They will try to intimidate you or butt into your relationship. But it's up to you not to allow anything to come between you and your husband, not comparisons, not manipulation, not thoughts, words, or actions. Once that ring is on your finger, forget the past and look toward the future. You are now the mistress of your house. Regardless of what the ex-wife tries, you are not responsible for her actions. You are only responsible for yours, and you can choose to be the bigger, more mature person. Practice forgiveness, or pity, or whatever you have to do not to harbor bitterness or anger toward her. If you do not make this practice a habit, that bitterness, resentment, and anger will eventually affect your marriage.

But above all, make a pact with God to pray for her. Every time something happens, grit your teeth and pray. And ask God to change *your* heart—that you would be able to show grace and love and that God would give you a strong heart and character to be God-honoring in circumstances beyond your control. Especially pray for the times when that person crosses your husband's path. Of course, it isn't easy. But your perseverance will pay off.

A Spiritual Investment

Several years before my marriage, I was visiting my grandparents. My grandfather had to work on Saturday morning and would be leaving around 6:00 A.M. For some odd reason—call it providence?—I awoke early. I went downstairs to use the "little girl's room" and paused at the family room when I heard my grandfather's voice. He was praying. I tiptoed by and glanced in, not wanting to disturb him, and stopped dead in my tracks. There in the family room were my grandparents kneeling by their recliners, praying for their marriage, for their day, for their family, for God's blessings. They never knew I was watching them, but that made an enormous impression on me. They've been married sixty years. I'd bet the farm those prayers are the reason.

My grandparents gave me a wedding gift that day even better than the fondue set they gave us on our actual wedding day. It was the gift of praying together. Scott and I made a commitment to pray every morning. Before we get out of bed, the first thing we do is thank God for the day, pray for the day's events, for our family, and for our marriage.

If your hubby doesn't want to pray with you, don't let that stop you from praying! God will still honor you for your faithfulness! It's always good to pray for your spouse privately, even if you do pray together as well. "Make a promise to yourself that you'll pray every day for your husband," says Eileen, married two years. "Pray that God will bless him in his work and health and relationships. And that God will protect and bless your marriage. What's great about praying for your husband is that because you and your husband are now united as one, when he's blessed, you're blessed in turn!"

Your marriage can't help but become amazing when you and your husband pray together. Make it a routine. It allows the two of you to be vulnerable in front of each other and God. It becomes a safe place to discuss issues and fears. It's the most intimate place you can be with each other. Trusting that the God of the universe hears you and your spouse talk to him will bring strength and miracles to your marriage.

Last Words: Better Off Wed

Now it's time to move forward into your new life. After all, as author Lowell D. Streiker writes, "Love starts when you sink into his arms and ends with your arms in his sink."[3]

My husband and I are still "newlyweds." And I'm pleased to announce that I'm even more in love with him than I was when I said "I do." We still laugh and tease. We have our private jokes and our secret signals. And scarily enough, we've begun to think alike. We still argue, and we're both still stubborn (although *he's* more so than I am). There are still moments when after a particularly heated "discussion," my mind will tempt me with thoughts of, *What have I done? I must have been insane to marry this person!* But when all is said and done, mostly I just spend much of my time looking at this man with whom God has blessed me and being struck with awe that God loves me so much that he gave me Scott. Those are the moments when my expectations have been exceeded far beyond anything I could have asked for or imagined. I pray the same great expectations are met for you in your married life.

Great Resources

Marriage Partnership magazine, published by Christianity Today International, 1-800-627-4942. Website: www.marriagepartnership.com (Sorry that this is a shameless plug of my magazine, but even if I didn't work for it, I'd still recommend it. It is a wonderful resource to keep your marriage on track.)

The Power of a Praying Wife by Stormie Omartian (Eugene, Oreg.: Harvest House, 1997).

The Power of a Praying Husband by Stormie Omartian (Eugene, Oreg.: Harvest House, 2001).

Beauty Restored by Me Ra Koh (Ventura, Calif.: Regal Books, 2001).

Birth Control for Christians by Jenell Williams Paris (Grand Rapids: Baker, 2003).

Inviting God to Your Wedding by Martha Williamson (New York: Harmony Books, 2000).

More Than You and Me by Kevin and Karen Miller (Colorado Springs: Focus on the Family, 1994).

Fit to Be Tied by Bill and Lynne Hybels (Grand Rapids: Zondervan, 1991).

Saving Your Marriage Before It Starts by Les and Leslie Parrott (Grand Rapids: Zondervan, 1995).

Getting Your Sex Life Off to a Great Start by Clifford and Joyce Penner (Dallas: Word, 1994).

A Christian Woman's Guide to Sex by Debra Evans (Wheaton, Ill.: Crossway Books, 1997).

Intimate Issues by Linda Dillow and Lorraine Pintus (Colorado Springs: WaterBrook Press, 1999).

A Celebration of Sex for Newlyweds by Douglas Rosenau (Nashville: Thomas Nelson, 2002).

Notes

Introduction

1. Robert Fulghum, *It Was on Fire When I Lay Down on It* (New York: Villard Books, 1989), 9.

Chapter 1 *You're Engaged! Now What?*

1. "Shine Language," *Mademoiselle*, November 2001, 117.
2. Linda Barbanel, "The Five Stages of Engagement," *Mademoiselle*, November 2001, 114.

Chapter 2 *First Things First*

1. Lisa Benenson, "The State of the Union," *Ladies Home Journal*, March 2003, 110.
2. Martha Williamson, *Inviting God to Your Wedding* (New York: Harmony Books, 2000), 157.
3. Ibid., 158.

Chapter 4 *Friends, Face-offs, and Free Advice*

1. Lowell D. Streiker, *Nelson's Big Book of Laughter* (Nashville: Thomas Nelson, 2000), 6.

Chapter 5 *Harnessing Your Inner Bride*

1. Douglas Rosenau, *A Celebration of Sex for Newlyweds* (Nashville: Thomas Nelson, 2002), 10.
2. Henri Nouwen, *The Road to Daybreak* (New York: Doubleday, 1988),157–58.

Chapter 7 *Countdown to the Big Day*

1. Richard Carlson, ed., *The Don't Sweat Guide for Weddings* (New York: Hyperion Press, 2002), 99.

Chapter 8 *Sex and the Single Girl*

1. Williamson, *Inviting God*, 84–85.
2. Heather Jamison, "Haunted by Premarital Sex," *Marriage Partnership*, Spring 2001, 24.
3. Amelia Clarke and Greg Clarke, *One Flesh: A Practical Guide to Honeymoon Sex and Beyond* (Kingsford, Australia: Matthias Media, 2001), 62.
4. Ibid., 62–63.
5. Kevin Leman, *Sheet Music* (Wheaton: Tyndale House, 2003), 37.
6. Willard Harley, *Buyers, Renters & Freeloaders* (Grand Rapids: Revell, 2002).
7. Me Ra Koh, *Beauty Restored* (Ventura, Calif.: Regal, 2001).

Chapter 10 *Last Moments of Being Nearly-Wed*

1. Lisa Skolnik, "Diary of a Bride," *Chicago Tribune Magazine,* January 2001, 22.
2. Ibid., 24.

Chapter 11 *Walking the Aisle*

1. Ilene Rosenzweig and Cynthia Rowley, "Throw a Storytelling Wedding," *Glamour,* February 2002, 63.

Chapter 12 *Fun Things to Do on Your Wedding Night*

1. Clifford Penner and Joyce Penner, *Getting Your Sex Life Off to a Great Start* (Dallas: Word, 1994), 16.
2. Rosenau, *Celebration of Sex*, 66.

3. Ibid., 52.

4. Louis McBurney, M.D. and Melissa McBurney, "Christian Sex Rules," *Marriage Partnership*, Spring 2001, 36–37.

5. Ibid., 37.

6. McBurney and McBurney, "Real Sex," *Marriage Partnership*, Winter 2002, 68-69.

7. Ibid.

Chapter 13 *The Honeymoon Hiatus*

1. Carlson, *Don't Sweat Guide*, 48.

Chapter 14 *What Do You Mean the Honeymoon's Over?*

1. Dan Zevin, *The Nearly-Wed Handbook: How to Survive the Happiest Day of Your Life* (New York: Harper Collins, 1998),163.

2. Fred Lowery, *Covenant Marriage: Staying Together for Life* (West Monroe, La.: Howard Publishing, 2002), 67.

3. Ann Platz, Susan Wales, *Social Graces for Your Wedding* (Eugene, Oreg.: Harvest House, 2002), 55.

Chapter 15 *Keep the Joy Alive—You're Married!*

1. Williamson, *Inviting God*, 166.

2. Lori Graham Bakker, *More Than I Could Ever Ask* (Nashville: Thomas Nelson, 2000), 246.

3. Streiker, *Nelson's Big Book of Laughter*, 248.

Ginger Kolbaba, a former editor at *Today's Christian Woman*, is now the managing editor of *Marriage Partnership* magazine. As a newlywed herself, she offers genuine understanding for brides from a fresh (and hilarious) perspective. She lives in West Dundee, Illinois.